D1594426

40TH CENTURY MAN
Selected Verse 1996—1966

ANDY CLAUSEN

By Andy Clausen

Poetry

Extreme Unction (Litmus) 1973 OP
Shoe-be-do-be-EE-op (Madness) 1975 OP
Austin Texas Austin Texas (Place of Herons) 1980 OP
The Iron Curtain of Love (Long Shot) 1985 OP
Without Doubt (Zeitgeist) 1990
The Streets of Kashi (Roadkill) 1995
Trek to the Top of the World (Zeitgeist) 1996

Recorded with Music

Blind Lemon Pozor & thelemonade (WE) 1991
Let It Rip by PoZor Spoken with Big Z (Zeitgeist) 1994

40TH CENTURY MAN

Selected Verse
1996—1966

ANDY CLAUSEN

AUTONOMEDIA

ACKNOWLEDGEMENTS

I remember this list of poems & versions of same appearing in these publications: "40th Century Man," "Big Apple Juice," "Way Out In You," *Boomana Press* (V. Stanbury); "Enkidu Returns," *Friction;* "Ahoj! Mr. President Ahoj!," Blind Lemon Pozor & thelemonade (tape), *We Press;* "Impressions of Titograd," *Long Shot* 11; "Uffizi Libatons," *Wordland Series;* "The Bear For Real/Electric Namche,"*Big Scream* 32; "The Streets of Kashi," Roadkill Press; "Goyko Lake," *Long Shot* 13; "Schopenhauer Never Got Here," *We Press* Broadside; "They Are Coming," *Without Doubt,* (Zeitgeist Press) & *New Directions* 37; "Ramona," *Without Doubt, Big Scream* 15; "Soldiers of Christ," *Without Doubt;* "Our Conceptions, Our Children," "WE 10," "The Toughest Bus Ride," *Trek to the Top of the World* (Zeitgeist). Back cover photograph is © Allen Ginsberg, Courtesy of Fahey/Klein Gallery, Los Angeles.

Autonomedia
POB 568
Williamsburgh Station
Brooklyn, New York 11211-0568

Fax/Phone: 718-963-2603
World Wide Web site: www.autonomedia.org

Printed in the United States of America

Contents

III. LATE 80's — BUDDHA, FUTURISM, NEW LOVE

IV. NEW YORK & SIBERIA

V. AUSTIN & DENVER & OAKLAND — WORKING FAMILY INTENSITY

VI. San Jose, Berkeley —
The 60's Gone — The Nixon Years

VII. Oregon & Alaska & Montana
& Canada — Up Country

VIII. Early Days — Psychedelphia & Leaving
Marines

To all my Friends
(Children included)
What courage you've shone
my Tomorrow

"Who am I?
I'm of no class,
no nation,
no tribe.
I've seen the Thirtieth
and the Fortieth
Century
I'm simply a man
from the Future."
Vladimir Mayakovsky, "Mystery–Bouffe"

I
PoZor Spoken
Love & Job Losing in the 90's

"I shall go by
dragging my burden of love.
In what delirious
and ailing night,
Was I sired by Goliaths —
I so large,
so unwanted"
Vladimir Mayakovsky, "The Backbone Flute"

"I'm a bluesman I love the blues
so much, I always have them;
they hang on me like arms"
Andy Clausen,"The Pozor Blues"

"Whatever it may be whoever it may be
The bloody man all singing all just
However he die
He rode on railroad cars
He woke at dawn,
In the white light of a new universe"
Allen Ginsberg, "Patna–Benares Express"

To Big Z, Hal Bright Cloud, Bruce Isaacson
friends when I needed them

40TH CENTURY MAN

Loneliness be my brother
together we'll walk alone
A back hoe is our mother
the lost highway is our home
You can't conjure what wasn't
The great & good aren't the same
Your sorrow gives life meaning
Deceit & love meet is the game
The truth may not be easy to swallow
but it's easy to understand
When you're a 40th
when you're a 40th century man

I've got some real gypsies
booming from the box
when they open their throats
& let those notes go from the bottom
It always gives me chills
I promise to play Hank Williams later
& hey don't drink too much with those pills

The huge wind sounds like motors
Rabbit's bark can't get clearer
This morning you shaved a fat

old stranger in yr mirror
Sick City deserts laugh at you
just as if they were human
Your face melts you reappear
Good morning Mister Truman
You got to want IT to understand
Life aint a bowl of cherries
When you're a 40th
when you're a 40th century man

I got some caravans
blasting from the deck
when they open their throats
and let those notes go from the bottom
It always gives me chills
I promise to play Rambling Man later
& hey don't drink too much with those pills

eggs are runny toast soggy
waitress lethal, she mumbles
spuds crumble, window's foggy
but the coffee's strong & good
like a pool table sans balls
Actor no clue to his cues
Like a prison without walls
not much for a boss to use
You got to want IT to understand
Life isn't a bed of roses
When you're a 40th
when you're a 40th century man

I've got the real Roms
clapping wild beats of old
when they open their throats
and let those notes go from the bottom
It always gives me chills
I promise to put on Elvis later
& hey don't drink too much with those pills

Oakland, 1994

SAME OLD SAME OLD

Ban violence on TV & legalize automatic weapons
Deny medical & education to immigrant free loaders
Will hire no questions asked & pay on merit system
What's the least you'll take?
How's a Big Mac an hour sound?
A lake a mountain a hunting lodge
A well earned US dacha? It could be yours
Forget who used to live here
What's the Statute of Limitations on Genocide?
End all profit cutting laws & socialistic
        funding of the EPA
Who needs water when you have money?
Money rides, money talks, all else walk
It's your choice: cancer protection clean
environment or a good old temporary job?
Quote the Bible, attest to Christ's
        Divine Superiority & Authority
And keep this nation's economy dependent
        on the manufacture & deployment of murder
While you're at it repeal the 1st & 4th amendments
Better X out the fifth commandment too
Register for the draft but if you're gay
        just don't say, in fact just don't do
In fact blame all societal ills on you
Pro-life is morally bound to kill
        legal abortion doctors

Kick unwed goldbricking mothers off welfare
Deny abortion rights, deny funds
Downsize business, give the penal system
        to the free market
After losing the war to make the world safe for
        democracy
The war to end all wars
The war on organized crime
The war on poverty
We WILL win the war on ersatz victims
We WILL win the war to make the world safe
        for techno-feudalism
And the weapons won't just be the purse strings
        not just a hunk of bread
        but real rifles tanks & bombs on the Internet
The world will belong to Mickey Mouse
Our History Snow White Fantasia Beauty & the Beast
They'll try to convince the whites
Natives are cartoon ughing scalpers
        with little or no language
African Americans are Hekyl & Jekyl
        or Cannibals making stew
Jews have horns, they'll try to make
Michelangelo's stupid mistake a reality
Boys Town will deal with inner city
Bing Crosby will save America's youth
Walter Winchell Joe McCarthy J. Edgar Hoover
John D., J.P., Nixon, will be victorious
It will seem like home
It will feel like home
The same old same old

Hayward, 1995

MORE SAME OLD

Why order us do what you can't & won't do
       for yourselves?
Why make us eat excrement to eat food?
Why make us breathe poison in order to secure shelter?

from the Adirondacks to the Gulf of Mexico
from Detroit's broken promise to someone else's
       private Idaho
from Fort Apache to where children denizen skid row
Where is there somewhere left for us to go?

Why talk to us like we're spit?
Why never satisfied with what we give?
Why demand we labor to destroy all we've learned?
To kowtow & grovel to get a fraction of what
       we've already earned?

Used to say it's a free country?
New motto is no new taxes
More interested in *anything* than us
Making money from Tehran to Texas
Promoting more barriers twixt the sexes
change worlds words health & welfare with
       lightening faxes
I think you'd kill Indians again just for a cut in taxes

from coast of Maine to the Gulf of Mexico
from Detroit's broken promise to Christian Identity's
          private Idaho
from Bed Stuy to where children denizen skid row
Is there somewhere left for us to go?

Hayward, 1995

ENKIDU RETURNS TO THE DEEPNESS
OF THE DEEP FOREST

A Vacana

O electric eddy of breezes
O plum heavy branch
O stars that cooly massage pristine
        happy faces of true youth
        with brilliant timeless extensions
Be-bopping reincarnated dakini birds
        riffing through the black blooded
        rips in the sky
I plead to you : Give me one gift:
        If you see my love
If you see her anywhere
The One more sparkling beautiful
        than thronging kaleidoscopic gems
        whirling with our sun
        dancing the Lake of All Memories
Yes, the One that you know so well
        the One you've blessed & endowed
O All of you; I beg, I beseech
If you see her If you hear her
Call out & show her to me
I! who have lost
I who have lost her
        implore you
Call out & show her to me!!

Oakland, 1994

I Should Join Up

I don't want to be Kropotkin ending his days
    freezing in a mansion with enough fuel
        to inadequately heat one room
so the bolsheviks can say look at the anarchist
    prince we've housed him in splendor
I don't want to be a feeble old man
    not even Emma Goldman can save
I'd rather perish in the woods
    be eaten by wolves and birds
    before giving up freedom of the press
I don't want Tom Paine's death
    with a 70 year old virgin standing
    over my death bed commanding
    "Repent Tom Paine Repent" over & over
    because I wrote *The Age of Reason*
I don't want what Dalton Trumbo, Frances Farmer
    Howard Fast & Walter Lowenfels got
I don't want to be Reich villified
    as a harmful nut
Hardhats marching to destroy my work
    my home my ideas
rejected by Hitler by Stalin by Truman
    for preaching orgasm
I should write ideas for people
    who live exclusively in books
    devote my life to culinary arts
        or astrology or ballistics

I should learn and practice every form
    of vassalage
work 8 hours watch television 4 hours
    shop 4 hours and sleep the rest
I should take to heart how outnumbered I am
    & realize when they say I have free will
they mean I am free to do what they want
           period.
I should take to heart their motto
    Freedom is not free
I should break all my be-bop records
    time has shown they will
        only get me into trouble
I should sell off my beat generation lit
    sell off my Marx and Godwin and Spinoza
    dismiss my Crazy Horse & Spartacus
I should just be happy I have a job
    and shut up
I should be a what me worry model citizen
I should kneel and worship dead men
    filling my pockets with dead inventors
I should join AMWAY

Oakland, 1977 & Hayward, 1995

BIG APPLE JUICE

My mojo's in escrow
& I owe John the Conqueror 5 dollars
Manhattan's all aglow
In the rear view my eyes flat fish out of water
The Williamsburg Bridge
my only friend we aint much but just like me it's free
But I guess that's show biz
How come they call Gem Spa a spa? It's a mystery
The Plaza Hotel is
like a movie set for an old large royal class
It's like the parties where
no one does/ thank fate & ass my heart's not that caste
Brooklyn Bridge is more
remarkable than World Trade centers ever can be
O Yes, Coney Island is more
relevant than all post modernity

Big Apple, gwine take a chance
        & dance and smile in Grand Central Station
                drink your juice
Get a job in a tall building
        steal millions of dollars
          & the Golden Goose
Big Apple, gwine drink your juice

5 years New York Woman
she making me believe my time aint long or dear
a stunning woman
Her mind's a revengeful table turning career
She taught me to scold friends
made me read Collette & French Feminist Writers
To change the means & ends
& I slept next to her months for a one-nighter
Yeah, gwine be cold heart
Look out for Apple One, New York love is drama
Did my part, played the mark
riding the subway ghost I aint got no karma
Garbage truck a crowing
The sigh reens beckon me row my stone boat
         down stream
All you should be knowing
is if you have talent take it to the double X-treme

(*Repeat First Chorus*)

The rad son & daughter
have to seek new turmoil, find old tribulation
No rain there's no water
Born to a tournament of utter frustration
Mechanic cross the street
can't get it together fix his whining starter
Raw tempers grill the heat
Bumper sticker sez I voted for Jimmy Carter
Bottle picker dumpster
It's time you change your mask, change your entire
         disguise

Lacklove streets gain bodies
with dislocated eyes, burnt, so WE can be wise
Thank the fool & doubter
You're not the only one to ever lose so bad
All ready knew bout her
You're not the only jerk threw away all he had

Big Apple gwine take a chance
            dance & smile in Grand Central Station
                  drink your juice
Get a job in an uptown gallery
            wait for problem free
            old girls to seduce
Big Apple, gwine drink your juice

Oakland, headed for NYC, April 1994

WAY OUT IN YOU

In your eyes I see what no eye can see
   to call it good would be nothing
In your eyes I see perfect use for my body
In your walk how you walk
   a reason there won't always be war
In the way you lift your cheek bones
   exposing the fragility & corruption
   of the stern & puritanical
In your little victory big smile
   something that can't be censored
There's a way out in you
   a way out of the Depression
   a way out of manic Loneliness
   a way out of stone grief
   a way out of here
   a way out of yesterday & year
   a way out of here
There's a way out in you

I saw the planet saved by the way
   your lip moved
No drug do a better job
   postponing my inevitable demise
like your eyes bright shining yes
   sparking the future

Magnificence that needs no utterance no fee
Beautiful satisfying beyond reproach & sin
Light from within & a way out side
I want to go with you
O Eyes of the Life I think I've forgotten
but never known, take me to the Pure
Dakini Land, Eyes, touch me again
There's a way out in you
   a way out of one dimension
   a way out of Armageddon
   a way out of impotent craving & raving
   a way out of here
   a way out of yesterday & year
   a way out of here
There's a way out in you

Oakland, 1994

THE LOVES I LOST

The loves I lost were beautiful
The loves I lost were great
My mother's love twisted
& sincere as the 20th century
I have a photo reproduction
of my biological father
who I never knew after 4
& an ocean between
My stepfather was a very tough man
affection in our household was
scarce & dirty
at least he was there
I was reminded a thousand times

My wife was the love of my life
but the hard life I was bent on
    killed her love for me
and my ability to really love
anyone was compromised
by my cowardice which kept
me from admitting it
Now I'm 50 years old
that's more than half over for sure
and I wonder about this concept

this emotion that has tortured me
and turned me into a strange being
this love this elusive feeling
that has produced all these inferior
other ones
I did not heed
I knew I heard I'd been hipped
One always says they're sorry
when it's too late

Oakland,1993

BEAST

I've seen this before, young & old
hanging out in the street
Except it's a side street, no business here
not even a liquor store
It's a weekday, it's midday
The group covers an entire block
Some say it's the westside
Other's say the east
The toughest always lose
It must be the Nature of the Beast

I've been here before, mother's eye me
suspiciously
My beard, hair, my complexion look like
killer of 12 year old girl
The drawing in the paper on the tube
I don't want to kill anyone
from the most powerful to the very least
The tension makes losers of us all
It just must be the Nature of the Beast

Feeling like a grand old cause
an old idea no longer needed
To have a grand hello
a smile for the streets

Puts one in margins
Marks one for invaders
We are not a people
We are not a nation
We're a thirst for sand
The workless pain is the real pain
Workers suffering, Bosses feast
The toughest always lose
It's just the Nature of the Beast

Oakland 1993–94

LOST

like Botticelli was worthy of Spring
I would be worthy of you
      leaving something that will endure
How vain to think I could
      beastly weak embroiled sad I
          could make words endure
exquisite, heartfelt & intelligent
      inhabiting the air ordinaries
      of all orders breathe & suffer
and a thousand years from now
      they would smile
          and rejoice that we lived & loved
and when for that moment I was I
      knowing my love for you was unconditional
          was the Dharma, Maitreya lives
      a perfect flower inside a drop of rain
          no longer without you
      no longer a slave to this pain
You who are to me more than anything
      I can ever write or say
more precious
      than all I have
          when you're away
brighter than the sun
sweeter than the day
more precious
      than all I have
          when you're away

Oakland, 1993

PHONE WITH MOM

My mother in mild despair rues
  my dearth of financial success
(her only criteria)
Mom, I'M BORN NOT FOR MONEY
  just like the Mayakovsky movie
  version of Jack London's *Martin Eden*
(I went for the glory, not the bread)
What will you do when you get old?
   Jack London will not help you
   when you get old. He is dead. You
   have no woman; who will take care
   of you? When I think how smart you were
   You could have been a lawyer, anything!
   You could have made something of your life.
Mom, now listen, and listen close, do you know
   in 100 years people will be studying your
   life & know why? Because you were *my* mother.
You sure think a lot of yourself
I'm trying to be objective
Well, tell me something, has your writing improved?
I think so, I'm learning & developing all the time
Good, I could hardly read it before.
   It was like cat scratch.

Oakland, 1992

ACCESS US!

Beauty is not dead
A Vision for the Future
        better not be dead
Romance & Love are not dead
Heart seeking description
Windows of mountains streaming
        resolve & wisdom are not dead
Battered old rattlers
Lovers of old objects
        that created yesterdays
        free of pain
        are not dead
Defiant traditions of straight talk
        on the life & death walk
        are not dead
The great paintings & parties
        in the verses of poets
        beyond language, awe inspiring
        felt in the middle of the body
        ZAUM is not dead
The Beauty of folk poetry
        is not dead
Only the Past

Only the vacuous language of obscurant
    academes writing only to impress
    other poets promoting exclusion
Only the nihilist TV heads
Only the fascist cowards
Only those who want knowledge to be
    private property
    are dead
Access Us!

Oakland, 1992

REGULAR DAVE

He's weeping his hometown is gone
the people the houses they're all gone
You're consoling him; you've got a new town
       a perfectly good town
Where anyone can make it with hardwork
"Just create your own job"
His culture, his language?
Cultures & languages die
They died before and they die now
What's wrong with one tongue anyway?
What's wrong with understanding each other?
What's culture anyway but lies used to preserve
       isms of malintent
You tell him come on laugh, work, pray
       find the One True God
He looks at you like disgusted
It's not a pose
He whispers to you: DO YOU KNOW WHAT
IT'S LIKE TO GO TO THE PLACE
       YOU SPENT MOST OF YOUR LIFE AND SEE IT ALL GONE?
TO NOT UNDERSTAND THE LANGUAGE OF THE NEW REGIME
TO KNOW YOU CAN NO LONGER STAY, TO KNOW
       IT NO LONGER EXISTS?
You say look I'm busy, it happened long ago, we'll
       have to get together, don't forget to vote no on yes.
So Regular Dave goes about his Biz, says to himself
       IT WASN'T SO LONG AGO

Oakland, 1992

This Notion

Just a failed code hero, that's me I admit
What's a failed code hero?
Well it's kind of like Ernest Hemingway
        you construct a brilliant code
               for how a man should act
and failing the impossible
        execute yourself for sacrilege

So I know I've failed by not executing myself
        no rifle in mouth
no hanging after writing in slit wrist blood
            not jumping off a bridge in Minneapolis
            losing at Russian roulette in Moscow
            a triple overdose
            exploding the paths to the heart
So why not I? Why not yet?
I have failed my code, ask my former lovers
        catch me in the morning, or at night
Seems part of the code I fashioned
from what I was offered was that the code
        was all right and to end it in what is
            called suicide is a violation
            of *that* very tenet
        a vilest disrespect of the code
A part, a very important part of the code is
        "it's not over til it's over"

The truth is, I don't exclusively blame myself
            for all my failures
The truth is, I can't let the dirty rat lice
            have what they want
The truth is, I just don't like the way it reads
            He killed himself
and the pieces of dung don't even care
It's just more proof their system works
            it bothers my sense of—well—
I don't know what to call it right now
                but it bothers me anyway
                        this notion
                that is useless
                        this notion
                that It is useless

                                        Oakland, 1992

SEND YOU BACK

"We're going to send you back to Belgium."
"There's no baseball in Belgium."
"You can't get along with your brother
and you cause trouble between your mother & I."
I'd been bad arguing with my 4 year old brother
    over a 3 inch high army and their battle
    formations.
I cringed in bed without supper, thinking
"Back to Belgium, where people are poor
    and don't eat hotdogs or burgers. There
    are no NY Yankees, no Oakland Acorns,
    no Milton Berle, no blue jeans, no friends
    in Belgium."

3 years later, I'm 11, a big weekend fishing trip
    with dad, into the Mother Lode Sierra.
I wake to hear mom and dad going at it.
I got up and pleaded "stop it stop it don't
    ruin the adventure!"
Mom's going crazy yelling things I don't understand
Dad's hissing in disgust.
Mom yells "André don't go with him. He's not your
    real father. He will drown you!"

All I could say was "Hunnh?"
Dad who wasn't my father rose from the couch
"Damn it woman, now you've done it. You
horse's ass you."
The fishing trip was off.
There was yelling for hours & spitting "Petain"
There was lots of Old Crow.
There was threats of suicide, telephone calls
        to friends seeking a lawyer.
There was that terrifying word divorce.
I'd hear 1000 times again.
but I wasn't sent back to Belgium
every attempt at suicide failed
every divorce never happened
and I went on with my life
and attempts at suicide failed
I have one divorce
(not even remotely funny)
I ate hotdogs and watched major league
baseball come to my home town
and never threatened to send my kids anywhere.
But I did visit Belgium and sat on my biological
father's grave, they have great french fries
in Belgium but they don't call them that
they call them apples of the earth fried
and they call soccer football.
have the best beer & strawberries
and all of Europe makes jokes about them
about their yokelism

Oakland, 1990

II

PoZor Buddha — All Over
the Planet

"All over the planet, people are understanding
  beginning to say: It's not working
  WE NEED A CHANGE"
    AC, "What Has Not Worked"

"I could settle down and be doing just fine
when I hear an old freight rolling down the line
    I hurry straight home and pack
because if I didn't go I believe I'd blow my stack"
      Hank Williams, "Rambling Man"

To Katie Hetts, World Traveler, Fire Fighter & Ecologist

AHOJ! MR. PRESIDENT, AHOJ!

The playwright philosopher president
    comes backstage
Only 2 bodyguards?
One with a long pony tail?
There's Pivo & more back here
We're celebrating in czech english japanese
Allen introduces us
Yes I have a question,
"What incentive? Where are you going to
 get the incentive for the workers
 to leave the pub & go back
 to jobs & factories?
 to do their direly needed best
 at 7-8-9 in the morning
 at 11-12-13 they are getting tanked
 their desire is kaput
 their guilt obnoxious."
"Spiritual Incentive,"
Allen & Anne are synchronized.

The president is tired,
"But you see, unfortunately, I have been
in prison for the last 5 years. That is why

       people must tell me."
My brain is gasping, "O my God, is this man
    a Myshkin, a saint, an innocent?
    a nice guy intellectual who likes Ken Kesey
    Lou Reed Frank Zappa Allen Ginsberg
    & Democracy? It's not a game! "

When will I ever have the chance to have the head
    of a nation listen to me again?
"Mr. President, I go to work I have to work 8 hrs.
 I work all 8, going, going, going, cranking,
 hump, humping, humping, always go. It is mind
 and body; I have no time to dream poetry
 and weeping in museums. Boring, dangerous, weary,
 then Pivo, not Pivo before work, no Pivo
 at work or I am fired. No house, no car, no food.
 I must fear too much."
"You are telling me all the workers
    are drinking in the pub? "
I see by his face this is a depressing notion.
Allen's already told him about the 100 years
    remaining for the planet
about censorship in the USA
about the dying forests,
the potential Chernobyls of the future
about candor ends paranoia
& how Czechoslovakia could benefit
    from meditation practice

Now too late, after rapping at you half smashed
I realize the Communists have said Pivo
    is Czechoslovakia's second bread

The workers will not be denied Pivo
   & the workers are the Party's Strength
It's been going on at least 30 years
Longer I'm sure
Pozor Pivo Ahoj, Pozor Pivo
Attention Danger Too Much Beer Too Much

The second bread
The second breath
The second wind
The second death

Ahoj!
Mr. President!
Ahoj!
Pozor Pivo Pozor!
Ahoj!

Prague, 1990

IMPRESSIONS OF TITOGRAD

then we're routed through Titograd
now this one's grim & ugly
absolute utilitarian decayed stagnant
bleak depressing suppressing, poisoning
    strength & initiative
    with a glance & wince
this train station dirty low down surly
this hamburger ancient juiceless carcass
    grindings, stale plain bun
this composting sauerkraut & fermented
    beet salad is disgusting
these early morning trashed cantankerous
    legions of chain smoking men
    are rough & smelly
women are not respected here
they're supposed to be workin
    or making babies: one.

The restrooms stink, the eastern style
    squat toilets are dying
the pollution is in the people's skin
    sweating industrial effluvia
the litter shameful

it's obvious it'd be like looking
    for a family untouched by death
    in a place like Benares
    to find someone here who had
    the hope to give a shit

It's a big drunken lifeless party
    lasted 40 years without
    a sobering
here there's no morning after
there's just the grave & this …
a lad about 12 years old
with a couple buddies on train platform
"Am I from England? No. U.S.A. You speak
good english."
"I have been to Brooklyn."
(Our train to Belgrade is approaching)
"Which do you like better?" I ask.
"Brooklyn or Titograd?"
"America" he answers, "100 times"
and though I can name a thousand things
I hate about life in the USA
(that's my problem)
I agree with him, this surely can't be
    what Marx & Engels envisioned
this nasty, grimy, desolate, dreamless
    uniform poverty & despair
this sacrilege & suffering
this drunken nightmare

Budapest Museum of Fine Arts
Goya's battle scenes are dark like tornado weather

people actually get killed in his paintings
ordinary people, not soldiers, not religious martyrs
they happen me, my neighbors, my family
and the weather sucks … !

Titograd & Budapest, 1990

UFFIZI LIBATIONS

Step right up, folks, we got it right here
in the Uffizi, for only 5,000, that's right
5,000 lira, that's 4 US dollars, the best,
the very best of the Italian Renaissance
& then some, we got Da Vinci Michelangelo
Raphael Mazzola Fromenti El Greco Goya
Reubens & Old Rembrandt too—

I spend an hour with my favorite: Botticelli.
Venus & Spring, slowly weeping, slowly
        smiling, either one with a shift
        of the body
There is so much to see, so much super
        star art, overwhelming
The devoted assiduous fervid religiosity
        crucifixion upon crucifixion
each one a bucket of samsaric tears & blood
hundreds of annunciations, depositions,
madonnas, gethsemanes, gabbathas, epiphanies,
calvaries, Bethlehems, Lazarus raisings,
the sinners Adam & Eve, ascensions,
assumptions, like a huge contest
who will paint the ultimate empathetic

   agonizing Good Friday?
the sweetest saddest Last Supper?
the prettiest uncorruptible Madonna?
The most sorrowful tender Pieta?
3 hours walking, pausing, studying,
     scribbling notes

& then, what is This?
Bacchus! Yes, it's you!
wearing your goofy hedonist pagan smile
mirthed in obsidian shining joyful
     good grief relief!
O Carravagio much bruised blood is eased
my back released from pious bondage
eyes drinking dazzling rings
     in the full wine glass
This wine is not suffering blood
     not consecrated ceremonious
     wee swallow
This wine is wine
irreverent shimmering endless wine
to make one pink cheeked tipsy
a high gypsy romantic as a harmless lech
way down loose like a stampeding moose
fulla heathen juice————Yes!

& what is this?
More relief, more release!
More high legged dancing merriment
     cajoling friends & lovers
new friends, new lovers, adventure
     & abandonment!

church is done!
school is out!
work is over ...
Jan Miense
A Scene In The Tavern!
This is not a scene from the Bible
This is hip secular copious indulgence
This is Freedom!
Long live the Transitory!
Eternity love these fleeting moments!
Love us, your temporary children
swimming in the actions of time
unholy desirers sweating carpe diems
in fermented air kicking our legs high!
We judge ourselves!
and the verdict is: Not Guilty!
Long live Exuberance! Now & Forever
          without goodbye
The verdict is: Not Guilty!

Firenze, 1990

What Impressed Me Most

During their ancient traditional afternoon break
Greece is riveted to subtitled american soaps
Never saw so many lemon, orange, & olive trees
Azure waters white houses red tile roofs
Sheep craggy aretes, ten thousand postcards
Old urns romantic poets oded
The beehive tomb of Agamemnon at Mycenae
place where he was by his lover
death stabbed
High fortresses on the rugged dry tors
where I relive Persian invasions
But what in all Greece impressed me most?
The labor & size of the great canal of Corinth
The Calcutta-like poverty of the Gypsies
living by the dumps in Patras
But most of all the pious devotion
of those faces glued to
"As The World Turns"

Patras, Greece, 1990

The Bear for Real

Rishikesh is clean for small Indian City
True you will witness pigs wallowing
        in used oil & automotive grease
Cows & dogs roam the streets turning garbage
        into patties early morning casteless
        workers gather
An occasional buff pulling a load of material
Bold monkeys in the alleys & rooftops
Big fish & birds in & about the relentless Ganges
But here comes the unexpected, wild & crazy,
        down the narrow street
A bear, a 250 lb. near extinct
        long snouted Himalayan bear
on a rope held by a 130 lb. man
        like it was a frisky dog

People scatter, give it wide passage
Katie wants to take a picture
He offers to bring his wild pet closer
She scatters, "no, no, keep it away, no closer"
I can't move, totally fascinated
The rope's not that thick, a big string really

51

passed through the bear's nose
At least it doesn't look frayed

Katie's back to try for the picture
He offers to bring it closer again
She scatters
I'm mesmerized standing there
He jerks the painful rope
"You want to see bear dance?"
The bear growls hugely bitterly
        rising up to dance two legged
        roaring anger & pain
Katie wants to know how much to give
I say I think 10 rupees
He has the bear sit & do begging
        motion routine
It's all done with the painful rope
Amazing
How does he feed it? & what?
Where do they sleep?

Katie's bargaining with him from afar
        offering 5
He says the bear wants 10
"I'd give him 10. He has the bear."
He gives the bear slack in her direction
"No 5, no 5, He want 10. "
        nodding to the bear.
She's brave or stubborn?
Tells him 5 or nothing.
He takes it & both are down the street.
"I just had 5. No change."

"Oh"
People give them the street
They stop & pose for one last photo
50 yards away

I'd been 6 or 7 feet from the bear
It certainly wasn't courage
It may have been stupidity
but I was stoned
the bear is my patron animal
I wrote a long poem entitled
    THE BEAR, so, yes,
I was stoned by the bear
I was stoked

O the snake woman & her large python
    crawling on her blanket
    next to her leg kicking infant
    I won't go near even if it's opiated
but was I impressed by that rare big
    white-snouted Himalayan bear
painfully led around by its nose
    thru the streets of Rishikesh
There's not many left
    big old angry bear
    on a rope thru its nose

Rishikesh, 1990

THE STREETS OF KASHI

high walking historical alleys Godaulia
& out to frazzling congested streets
in tea & kirkidum shops over ghats
rickshaws, tuk-tuks, buffalo & throngs
come here to die or be reborn
on the Streets of Varanasi, Old Benares,
the Eternal City, Kashi

Left over garbage eating cows in the 2 cow wide alleys
Big Brahma bulls like they ride in the rodeos
Pigs & goats, it would seem, run free
Brick & cement carrying mini-donkeys hustle
through the alley of pilgrims
A dry cement covered young boy switches them onward
Men & women pass water against walls, in gutter
ontop of dung piles
Ever colorful poor Rajastani pilgrims far
from their everything brown desert home
amazed like hicks in NYC
Bharangi women scrape all fresh manure into washtub
size pudding like piles, their hands form it
into patties pasted on buildings & slopes
facing the sun
And Ho, Wombi, Wombi Baba, Ho!

There's wild crazy off beat funky honking happy
goof parade music coming thru the alley
towards the ever popular Ganges
and behind them a corpse with a golden sheet
& fresh garlands, being portered to the Torch
& here's a white sheeted one

7 ablaze at once, 4 or 5 waiting
All day long, O Happy Day
Look there's a little one can't be more than 5
Look at the scantily clad chandals heave bodies & logs
See them carry baskets of ash on their steady heads
See their bare feet cracked with dried blood
See their well defined leg muscles
Manikarnika Ghat
Where it all goes into the Sacred Ganges
the devout bathe & puja, sing the day-glo orange dawn
drinking mouthfuls of the waters,
with their brahmin cords, beautiful brass bowls & soap
next to where the sewer pipe washes up
visible dead rats & everything else evacuated by night
into the Sacred Ganges, It All Goes

buffalo carcasses float sink & wash up
boatloads of human ash
Dhobi wallahs beat clothes clean on special
flat rocks, ankle deep in Ganges
Giant unheard of river porpoises arc out
of the river like Loch Ness monsters
Lines of cripples, self-amputees, hapless
"scheduled "families, dozens of lepers are shouting
"Look at me! Look at me!" holding up their stumps

Unhappy women hold their listless babes in the air
as we walk by as if they were Eucharists

Everyone here already knows me
"Hallo," they want to shake my hand
"Change money? need guide? take rickshaw, take boat,
sir, I am boat man, come to where you don't want
 to go, no, I take you, 10 rupees, OK, 8, You want
 something? What you want?"
"Yes, peace."
"Come to my guru, one time, he give ayurvedic medicine
 just 10 minutes, you pay what you want. Perhaps
 then we look at my uncle's silk factory? "

It can take more than 5 no's
It can take more than instant catatonia
Any discussion gooses the hard sell
have tea, contribute to the school they need
to start up so the kids will grow up Christian
look at silk, look at this, they pull,
they scream all at once
If you do want something or show interest
there's a dozen on you

everything is a game, all is illusion
and illusion is all
everybody talk as loud and fast as possible
They'll say the lodge you want is full
out of business, flooded, anything
They'll peddle you miles the wrong way
before admitting they don't know the way
Every fare an argument

Head massage 2 rupees?
They'll go for shoulder it'll feel good
then the body & it'll cost more than 2 rupees
A leper tries to climb in the rickshaw
to touch you to coerce bhakshish
Walking trees of flutes, ah, he plays well,
you've weakened, he's on you, other flute trees
are descending, arms of beads, human malas
You yell, they yell louder, they come
as your saviour, "Benares, too much sell, sell.
Tourists come here to relax. What country? "
"U.S.A."
"Oh, is very nice country. Come with me
 to my uncle's silk factory. We'll have some tea."

back to bhang lassi corner, the most hectic
the lassi wallahs are yelling & waving their wet hands
they really do know me
sitting in the shade downing 3 strongs
watching the incredible sweltering saga
of laughable suffering humanity managing life
on the pandemonium streets of an over crowded
insane asylum, a holy city

A cop with lathi stick struts over pushes me
back down, anxiety is a word, so's paranoia
He just wants to shake my hand
3 strongs, yes!
Here's a drag faced leopard loin cloth
Shiva Baba with toy snakes attached to his hair
ankles, wrists & neck
Shiva Shiva, Shiva Shiva — Hey!

Here comes a baba wearing a pullover gorilla mask
Teenagers, old folks, all bananas
A gorilla!
We pass
Three steps later flabbergasted my voice softly
realizes, "That gorilla baba pinched my dick."

The Golden Temple is off limits to non-hindus
It's a sea of pushing shoving squeezing
non-stop devotion & cows run free
the bulls lose it, chase & body block whoever
it's karma

Up ahead people are walking around something
it's a man, early 20's, lying in the street
a little splot of puke by his ashen head
flies all over him, looks so sweet & angelic
so natural, all stretched out . . . . .

the waiter like so many others brings our glasses
with his fingers inside them
I think of all the left hands in India
The red spit pan just misses my sandal
3, 4, 5 pan stands to a block
little crowds around each stand
early in the morning the working class lines up
for their pan fix like an early morning 7-11
store scene by a construction site
going for the caffeine
Here it's betel nut & white lime & other esoteric
powders producing blood hued spit
in the back of the rickshaw we dodge

when the driver turns to spray it
crimson & black toothed
before dawn till the lights go out
as long as business goes on
the wallah wallahs catch it sliding
out of the big green leaves into their
hungry excited gums

A young leper is pulling another on a creeper wagon
They stop.
The one riding is noseless lipless & earless
half an arm, the other hand and both feet gone.
He rises up, sings loud & clear
some old indian hymn I reckon
The entire remains of his body quakes
loud robust notes
I fantasize: Ed Sullivan on his variety show,
"And now direct from Varanasi, India :
The Singing Lepers!"
that's worth a rupee or two, aint it, Ed?

On the banks of the Sacred Ganges
a young writer from America studies 3 Bengalis
One wants him to know, "Benares is very holy city.
God's city. For 10 million years........."
This Bengali raises his face to the sky
quivering with piety & awe,
"God!"

Varanasi, 1990

GOKYO LAKE BREAKING UP IN THE SUN

Is that the sound of 10,000 birds barking like mountains?
No.
Is that the sound of outerspace, the other-never-heard
   by-us-world?
No.
Perhaps then, it's 13 sacred cannons firing huge flaming
   balls of redemption in our Path?
No! No,
It is just Gokyo Lake Breaking Up in the Sun.

Is that an avalanche like sin punishment & emptiness
   unknown?
Is that a real avalanche a Loudness birthing Eternal
   Silence through its renting stone Cervix?
Is this the iron irony of molten medicineless
   miniscule buried alive Death?
No, Gokyo Lake is Breaking Up in the Sun.

Are these the whirring teeth of mechanical contraband
   come to take the high trees?
The motorbikes of Bangkok angry at the rushing
   minutes lost?
New York honking its collective gridlock worldwide?
Is it a freeway collapsing in my Home Town?

Is it the 5th Horseman?
No, listen, It is Gokyo Lake Breaking Up in the Sun,
    listen!

Has the Ganges decided to flow into Tashkent & form
    a moat around Moscow before emptying into the
    freezing waters twixt Finland & Leningrad
    causing untold relentless havoc?
Has a monster finally found its Form?
Is Los Angeles about to implode thru the yak dung
    stoves?
Is it an Earth Quake?
A fierce revengeful Dakini I did wrong?
Is it all my previous had-to-be-horrible incarnations
    come up to vomit me into a hell
    only I could conceive?
No, It is only Gokyo Lake Breaking Up in the Sun.

What is this jade?
This ultra reflection vibrating liquid
    doing for free all a gem's intended to do?
My musings are vanquished by the Loudness
Has the mountain we walk on fallen in?
Have Sagarmatha's glaciers calved?
Has the sky storming herds of yak
    driven by reincarnations of murdered monks?
Has the colossal energy of might-have-beens
    self immolated like war heads
    along the crumbling ridge?
Has peace been broken like eggs in the nest?
Is that growl a genocidal demonic tractor or bulldozer?
No, In the Sun Gokyo Lake Breaks is All

Why are you not convinced?
Why won't you take the Answer?

What?   Aren't those tribal drums?
    multiplying?
Isn't there a bloody revolution in the bottom of my shoes?
Aren't gongs struck in my sentient temples?
Has the moon left for keeps?
Answer me!
What is that catastrophic coughing from a wounded lion
    large as Cho-Oyu?
Who is that wheezing far away man?

Hey You!
Those drums are the beatings of your heart
    older than its many moons
Those gongs are the clangorous reverbs
    of your locomotive lungs
Your money changer purged temples are filled
    with the blood of the masses
    of uncelebrated martyrs
That is your coughing & you are no lion
    shimi shimi
That wheezing far away man is just the sound
    of Gokyo Lake Breaking Up in the Sun.

A woman strong & beautiful drags you to the top
    for your audience
    with the Mother of the Universe.

Gokyo, Gokyo-Ri, 18,000 ft.
with big view of Sagarmatha (Everest)
Nepal, December 1989

On the Streets of Electric Namche

Tashi Delek
Katie talks to Tibetan Nomad Salt Traders
(they hold their newly acquired ropes)
She wants permission to take their picture
A local Tibetan merchant (Lhasa, originally)
   translates her Lhasa style Tibetan
   (she studied)
   into their rural dialect.

The Salt Traders are Wild
Exuding what I think some call ANIMUS
Untamed Light in their Dark Eyes
   my adrenaline mistook for fierceness
They are impressive like pages of mysterious history
   in their leathers & red string adorned wild
   dreaded hair & on-the-town grin
20,000 ft. Apache Cowboys on the precarious trade
   trails & passes linking Sherpas with Tibet
   a route routine hundreds of years

I'm watching respectfully 25 yards away
Standing on the small square in radiant thawing sun
4 French women in bright multi-colored new clothes
   materialize pirouetting & posing about discussing,

I think,
how their pants fit
all around me as if I were invisible
upon their clever stage

a train of zopkyos & yaks is hustled thru
the snow melting streets, leaving & going
Katie looks thru her lens at the dignified Tibetans
    posing, smiling, awesome

                              Namche Bazaar, 1989

THE TOUGHEST BUS RIDE OF MY LIFE OR JIRI-JIRI

Another all time list topper
12 hours of pain reserved seats in hell
passing through the forms of heaven
in order to sit straight ahead
the distance between knees & hips
would have to be less than 12 inches
the 25 inch waist Nepali guy
with the window seat got on too late
can't sneak in, if anyone moves,
that's the position they ride in
space vacated is unregainable
He decides to ride one knee on top
of each of two seat backs
If I wasn't looking at 12 hours minimum
with stories of 20 or 30 hour trips afresh
perhaps it'd be laughable & classical
The safety record is unsafe, I realize

Babies crying, upchucking on strangers
Huge gunnysacks of rice, sugar,
village supplies, chickens alive, kerosene
spilling, young & old spitting, hawking
bronchial oysters between badly cured

cigarettes, coughing like the T.B.
100 people space for 45
another 80 or so on top with the baggage
a company kid working the back door yells
sings & chants bangs the outside of the bus
as we cruise groups of bus riding prospects
"Jiri-Jiri, Jiri-Jiri-Jiri! "
(our destination)
He's crazy, he wants more passengers!
"Jiri-Jiri" like "Ice Cream, Ice Cream!"
or "Mecca, Mecca, bus leaving for Mecca! "
"Shet up, kid, Shet that kid up."
an already hurting Brit trekker pleads
to no avail

Halfway through the trip
Nepalis in the back begin shouting
"Manche muryo, Manche muryo!"
"a man is dead, a man is dead!"
Out the back window I spy the man mid-air
off the top of the bus, clears the top
of the wall, flips head over, quick
tumble and stop at big rock saving
him from endless rolling
the driver stops, an overlarge ad hoc
committee runs back, he doesn't have
a prayer, tears welling up, I know
this is adventure and all that but I
don't want to see people die
because a gallon of petrol costs
3 days wages and the bus must be full
like a depraved circus act

but he's up, walking, testing his legs
& arms. A long deep gash across his head
"I'm strong," he says.

And I said the bus from Chiang Rai to Chiang Mai
was too bad just because the driver used up
half his brake shoes barreling thru 50 miles
of winding hills till the entire countryside
was engulfed by the sickening smell
The driver's assistant handed out plastic bags
to everyone in event of sudden illness
but this bus to Jiri-Jiri takes the blue ribbon
I'm amazed at the pain we can all take
Where else can one live a 12 hour bus ride
up & down the steepest roads in the world
in an ancient arthritic terminal bus?
World Class narrow switchbacks
The Himalayas out the windows
negotiating irrational hairpins
the last 2 hours dim stuttering headlights
in moonless dark, where else?
Where else so much fun with the odds
catastrophes, rupees, caged space,
all of it, value?
All for under 3 dollars
I ask you, Where Else?

Jiri, Nepal, 1989

SCHOPENHAUER NEVER GOT HERE

She counts in Tibetan, almost like Akha
      they understand
Who needs to count past 100 anyway?
Why make problems?
Roosters crow 4 AM
Kids play rubber band lagging
   & shooting games
good shot: thumbs up
we understand
folks work the fields, the jungle
babes like everywhere want attention
sitting in skirt between legs of mom
Why do we need to know where it comes from?
    where is it going?
To suffer?
To earn more suffering?

Warts like clumps of grapes from ankle
    to the knee, can't be good
The lad is not self conscious
His face is not suffering
If I hadn't read those books
If I hadn't been made sick

    with vistas of accomplishment
    glory, leaving my mark
This is where I'd live
Air, Rice, Fruit, Family, the Poppy
    Dawn Again
    & Dawn Again
      Then Night

Golden Triangle, 1989

III

LATE 80's — BUDDHA, FUTURISM, NEW LOVE

" ...but the wild
            and the breath
        and the rage
            and the cure..."
Ray Bremser, "Poems of Madness"

"The Way is not the Way."
Lao-Tse

To the Wojczuks & Wards & V. Stanbury
Poets & Artists All

LUBLICKA

To have conviction, a body fluid zeal
    an unlimited desire to emit words
        till they are no longer words
    transforming Eternity & our place
        within it beyond Eternity
To find out what Eternity means now
To create scripture like Blake & Kabir
To outline glory like Whitman
To scribe with revolutionairy juice
    like Mayakovsky mobilizing
        modernizing the language
        of our homes
To trace baby camels in the sky
    Elana Guro
        I love you

The dream of what your reciprocation
    means
Keeps this oldening man
    safe from pity
In this I have not failed
    I love.

Oakland, 1988

OUR CONCEPTIONS, OUR CHILDREN

Concepts: The Iron Law, The Golden Eternity
    Diamond Cutter Sutra
as *words* depend on minerals for authority
    appeal, validity
for in practical sense without Iron what's
    Law going to do?
That is why it's the Iron Law
And without Gold, what's Eternity?
    just a long time.
    okay Golden's not a mineral
It's a quality, a color, yet Golden
    without Gold?
a colorless eternity is remote
white's too depressing, black impossible
even non-eternity is beholding to Golden
And the Diamond Cutter Sutra
    would it have influenced & nurtured
    The Asokan culture had it been named
    The Wheat Cutter Sutra or the Cutter
    Sutra or the Butcher Boy Sutra or the
    generic Sutra say Sutra No. 5?
without the jewels in the air
the lesson is still the lesson

this vehicle this compassion
 needs the wormy soil
the waters of life
 are water
the jewels in the eyes are of far more value
 than fancy stones & glittering alloys
the Law the Teachings, Eternity
 your skin against mine is more dear
 to me who holds up the cooking compost
as if it were precious
as if it were an Eternal Gift
 for us and what we grow this temporality
that gives us Eternity
 Is more than iron gold diamonds
 Is more than law teachings eternity
 Is more than the Past
After all what are all the Great Words
 compared to You & I?
Our Conceptions,
Our Children?

Boulder, 1987

Big Time Beaucoup Toke of Mighty Zaum

Infinite Zaum! Perpetual Future! Down Home Fuse
      Explorode!
Perpetual Motion Nightmares of Zaum!
Erectile Projective Blues Zaum! New Woman Muse!
Elevated Wrangle & Whang Dong DO Dangle!

Infinite Zaum! Reborn Beyonsense Be Re colored Bop
      rhythm
      of Transrational Transnational Bingo Lingo
      Zonga
      Zangezi Zappage Sand Doom Khartoumic Vast
      Folk
      Kicking Warm & Desperate E-motion & Co —
      Motion
straight out & back in, to go all the way is to begin
unborn imprisoned limbo marooned utters
the purge-a-torial blurry blue mumbles & guffaws
      from the center of each vowel & hand

Zaum sound of sweat triumphant
Zaum come in the flesh
Zaum lonely & lonesome
Behold it comes quickly

IT comes like effrontry on fire
Up off your knees!
Down from your throne!
Off your page!
ZAUM energy at last!

Beware you enemies of ZAUM
You will not be able to kick away
          beyond the windows in your high
muck muck cubicle of apres modern buck backed
          authority feasting on the frustration
          of the barrenness of all who will not
          service your "pre-destined superiority"
Your air conditioned nightmare: our nightmare
You will not hide in your books nor looks
          nor passports to access & excess
Your celluloid escape will shiver as it hears
          ZAUM chanting marching like a million
          forklifts & dump trucks
You'll in your spine feel the rattling
          of ten trillion dirty dishes
The produce of rattling road beat lungs
          will land on your desks
The unwashed will follow you home into your bedrooms
The breath of the animal you most abhor
          will singe your ears, the first smell of morn
You'll rise from your perfect paid for duffs
          and you'll scream and throw yourselves to
          the floor and claw and spit and weep and
          spasm about like fish out of water
          and you'll beg ZAUM for its love

Shoe be do be shoe be do shoe be do be means I love you
Boo-deee-apt, ZAUM orooni Mcvout Slam in the Jam
        of the Gam & Yam
Isn't art the mating call of Alchuringa?
Isn't poetry the cadence & trill thrill of Love's
        Billion Hearted Tragedy & Vindication?
Isn't philosophy really the blues?
Isn't mathematics the meter of molecular unity?
Isn't music the dress of the body's fluids?
Isn't ZAUM the salvation of the planet?
You'd better believe IT!

I know you want me to write like I did yesterday
I know you want me to write like I did in texas
        like I did in The Iron Curtain of Love
Don't get too drunk, don't get too excited
I don't understand what you are doing
Why all the blue talk & subjects
Why so depressing & bitter?
Your father says the sixties are over
        when will you realize?
Now you're trying to impress the people
        who rejected you?
The language poets & surrealists
ZAUM flat scats the street is not a language poet!
The tovarisch street pumps ZAUM
We are a hungry weed of electricity
        from the dark side of life

Down with your snob literature
Down with your self coddling & depreciating
        imposter art

Down with apathetic cruel politics
       excited only by money
Down with your programmed heart
Down with your blood & lymph stressing
       regurgitated syntax
Down with your lethal racist Aryan grammar
Down with your women hating fantasy war machines
Down with your love!

You will not hide in your wallets
You will not be safe in your restaurants
Your classrooms will climb out the window
ZAUM will come to end your power
ZAUM will be so much more than you've imagined
ZAUM is coming & your ersatz love is doomed
Infinite ZAUM!

Boulder, 1987

SWAMP

The old grey moss looks like fog
The ground looks like the overcast sky solidified
The shack's hodge podge boards termited terminal
The remnant window glass wears generations of sweat
The furniture has cancer donating last days
       to altruistic servicing of the dying commune
When we say crash we mean it out here
       in the swamp

It's like this: we started out with an idea
       we could change societal values
          in a few short years
We would do it by first changing ourselves
We would isolate ourselves from the mainstream
We really felt it was a spiritual emergency
We scoffed when others said it was just youth

Now we're the last ones and just pace the
       loose disintegrating floor boards
We know when we die all won't die
       ideas are more viable than flesh
O we're aware most will say ideas require flesh
       but admit real ideas are harder
          to come by than flesh

Okay this is the idea: all this suffering
       is not necessary
We have to just accept the beauty of the swamp
         the comfort of the terminal chairs
         the temporalness of buildings & flesh
         & the immortality of ideas
No we're not free to jump 100 feet in the air
No we're not free to touch our old loves
No we're not free of arthritic awakenings
No we're not free of our regrets
No we're not free of the limitations of substance
No we're not free of the blood hounds on our trail
No we're not free of time
But we're free to think to pace to sit to crash
       in our beloved swamp

Boulder, 1986

SEXUAL SURVIVAL
IN THE CHEMICAL DEATH FACTORY

a beauty of women arrive reflected
            in glittering shoes
the highly trained fingernails of the customary
            customers mark my unfair karma shuffled deck
                  dealt underhand & dead hearted
I'm to work this crowd, the united nations of my bod
            under going a famine of REMS
my knute rockne get up kid simon of cyrene
            walt whitman never say never pep talk
                  might as well talk to the wall

I conjure, like captured slaves their homes
            as they plan escape or revolution,
that wonderful kicked back unsmashed
            extasy little taste of softness
                  touching easy night so cool

so warm so right
2 or 3 times is enough
            for one night
all planned & ritualed or nonce
            it's wonderful

the sun more than kissing us
        going down and around
                the world on us.

I picture your pointilled outline
        your sparkling physicality
draped with serapes of fabulous tropic birds
        winging oblation for all our baroque
                positions, secreted satiated ever
                renewable roccocco coco desires
        wild born inside alphabets lambent
        like neon arabesque mystical motels
        that with unwitherable devotion
like inexhaustable crazy wisdom pilgrims
        pining the fleshed embrace of their Other
        embrace the tongue of the future
        with wet sexual lips

This I weave into the erotic gyrations
        of the now seducing eternity
blankets to soothe & cure my sleep raped will
This will comfort, this will keep time moving
This will expose the difference
        all those bon vivants extol
        with their jay taw dores and shut the doors
This will discern & surgerize the symbol
    from the semiotic, the seminal from the ephemeral
    and the funereal from me and enter the space we were
        the time on the desk the night in the shower
the time you said you were still wet days later
I run them by like after life projected
        epic movies in infinite resolve

ANDY CLAUSEN

to make it through another caustic
forever night of this despicable
deadend job
I'LL SEE YOU IN NEW YORK

Golden, Colorado, 1986

IV

NEW YORK & SIBERIA

"I have blasphemed
Screamed there is no god
but from the depths of hell
god led out a woman to make
the mountain tremble and shudder
and ordered, love her "
Mayakovsky, "The Backbone Flute"

"It is a hopeful augury of revolution that there should
be even now a formulated Declaration of Rights approved of
by a growing number of intelligent and resentful people, and
resisted, actively or passively, by every existing government on
earth. For governing gangs and classes every where know what
that declaration means for them. It offers a fundamental law for
a united and recivilized world, into which their pomps and
pretensions will be dissolved, and as an old order of things
become more and more plainly an intolerable confusion of
enslavement and frustration, it will be the sole means of unit-
ing and implementing a thousand storms of resentment."
H.G. Wells, *You Can't Be Too Careful*

To Eliot Katz, Poet, Activist
& Danny Shot, Poet, Teacher
& Alex Uribe, Sculptor, Builder
All Big Hearts

In Cleveland

I told you the legendary yet obscure beat jazz poet
      talked so dirty to this young woman she had
      to excuse herself & take a shower
And you said I know just the woman for him
as if that would solve all problems
Yes, you continued she's an alcoholic earth mother type
An alcoholic earth mother type I had to say it to
      understand it; I knew I had to find a real job
      soon.
Sure, you affirmed there's lots of them
I moved my uplifted brow
In Cleveland you added piously
They are like rusty roses you kept on
In Cleveland.
I looked in the want ads for my sanity
and chuckled about the movie
Revenge of the Alcoholic Earth Mothers
Sure we all know the type like rusty roses,
in Cleveland. Yeah alcoholic earth mother types
know them well.

Long Island City, NY, 1985

LEGS OF WINE

Woman, unhand my nipples
          it just won't work
stop humping & grinding my spine
my hand is beginning to cramp
          forget the salt tablets
And take that fucking exquisite
          everything unredundantly
          appropriate Mozart
out of the asparagus & lemon sauce air
this way fast & that way hard & deep & now
          I'm not a machine or toy
          & I'm sure as hell not your slaveboy
Yeah, I've snatched defeat from the jaws
          of victory with Blue Angel lust
studying the legs of wine & yours
          & your Marlene Dietrich face
and the money I blew
the sleeping with light on
          to enhance our dreams
and your interpretations
          forget it
if our love making isn't spontaneous
          then what do we have?
If you don't want to all out fuck me

then let me go
let me cry & get on with it
because this way of yours is killing me
why can't you just love me?

Milton, NY, 1984

THE DECONSTRUCTION OF AN ERECTION

Blue balled blue the fruit of desire flew
She expected me to drive 80 hard miles each way
        to the Apple for a deconstructionist salon?
I'm a construction worker & I have to work on Tuesdays
O she's interesting and good looking
She's so educated and refined and fine
I'm 1800 miles from the kids & their mom
I am very lonely

I have only a shovel to battle fire & flood
I feel like a potato or losing lottery ticket
I go from paycheck to paycheck
I read about billions for star wars defense
I drink beer and pee and so what
not even spit in the ocean
I feel like I'm drowning in a big brown river

Monday was a different sabbath
Friday night was a huge disappointment
I only see what's not here
I want that Great Instead
I couldn't keep the family together
I was an asshole under pressure
And you know what that means

Face it a laborer's not anybody
Calloused hands are not a good sign
The food picker's not prosperous
Health care is not for the poor
A woman's body is not hers
People like us have no say
when it comes to war
Reagan's 20 points ahead & gaining
We're not only oppressed
We're so stupid we vote for it
Alexander Blok walked around in the snow
        aimlessly. Mayakovsky asked him:
"Well, how do you like it?" (meaning the Revolution)
"The revolution's a good thing. I like it just fine.
        Oh, they burnt my library."
Sergei Yessenin used his veins to pen
his 4 line Ecclesiastes
Mayakovsky's bullet is lodged in my heart
like a white burn
Tsevetyeva's rope burns my neck
I can't write *Doctor Zhivago*
All I've done is rave to no avail

Soon all talk of peace will be treason
Soon this country will be Stalin's
Soon Hitler will be rehabilitated
This Reagan and his controllers
are just the beginning
Our protests are dust
Our art buried in apathy
Our defiance on the death bed

ANDY CLAUSEN

Nancy Reagan's china costs more
than a waitress can make in 10 years
Even if one reads the history of the planet
It's hard to fathom how it got this way

On the night of the 2nd Mondale-Reagan debate
I'm listening on the radio
Mondale proving he's not soft on Communism
states Che Guevera was a despicable person
(and I have to root for Mondale?)
Reagan's trying to prove he's a peace maker
and states he'll share star wars with the Russians!
I am bored to grief
I whip out the monster
and hit the cabin roof
picturing the deconstruction woman
in her salon, elegantly dressed
being so damn fucking smart
It must have flown five feet straight up
I think that's a new record

Milton, NY, 1984

Boddhisatvas All

The true decadents, boddhisatvas all
lurking in the burroughs
brothers of the far under world
with final failing spasms claiming
their sainthood with grey stubble
and purple lipped protest
the breath of a garbage dump
pocked and twisted blood busted faces
can't catch no freights
with rusted bones watching helplessly
as their friends fail to stand
Lives in default
each with a story, each with a name
boddhisatvas all

New York City, 1982

Jesus Horseback on the 4th of July

My eight year old son, Jesse, is explaining
       the drawing he's just executed
"Do you see it dad? It's Jesus snapping his fingers
       riding a horse celebrating the 4th of July!"
"Hmm, yeah, sure is."
I didn't tell you my Jesus remains a sad story
A good one goes early & dirty
Evil (I can't think of a better word) politicos
       have screwed the Jesus name & story
       everyway but loose
They've made the name a muse for war & tyranny
They've used the religion using his name
       to justify stolen property
They've used a belief system antithetical to his
       to put a pornographic stench on all beauty
They've equated favor with him with money

My Jesus dies a sad old man in Gorky
Maxim Gorky dies an unlistened to old man
       in Gorky
Mayakovsky takes the bullet
       on Mayakovsky Square
Martin Luther King dies
       on MLK Boulevard
Buddha dies as clueless would be buddhists
       worship his image

And God is murdered
            in church after church
Christmas is the celebration of hypocrisy
The 4th can be sad also
Thanksgiving, eating at peace with the original
            folks of America, after what was done to them
            bah humbug! Hypocrites!

Jesse hears me mumbling, "Dad what's a hypocrite?
            Is it somebody like a mean schoolteacher?"
I don't know how to answer that.
Reminds of the time when you were 4 listening
            to Waylon Jenning's Ramblin Man
You asked, "Dad, what's a rambling man?"
The words went "don't mess around with any old
            rambling man"
You wanted to know, "Why can't you mess with one?
            Is it like a robot? Is a rambling man in-
            destructible? Can he breathe fire? Does he
            have bad bad weapons?"
I knew then you were destined to ask tough questions
And I'm going to try to answer you here in our
            pleasant & rugged exile called the Committee
            on Poetry in Siberia New York at least 25,000
            miles from the Stray Dog Cafe
"Son, a hypocrite is someone who wants you to do
            what they don't won't do themselves or
            who condemn you for doing what they do
            but won't own up to."
"Oh, cheaters & liars?"
"Yeah."

                              Siberia, New York, 1981

WATCHING MY BREATH
IN CHERRY VALLEY, NEW YORK

Kicking back belly stuffed lazy as a big cigar
I'm a gargantuan zucchini in the watered sun leaving
        garden
a babe on a breast curled up cooing both hands on it
my eyes lost in panoramic golden fields
unexpectedly exquisite purple potato flowers
giant burdock like elephant ears
the forest beyond 40 shades of green
and the smells! the maples, the rhubarb, the wild
flowers & strawberries, even the manure pile

Not a machine to be heard, not even a distant car
no planes, no televisions, no neighbors squabbling
no chainsaws
Watching my breath, not guilty
Watching my breath, impervious to all advice
Watching my breath, ridding myself of crusades
ridding myself of anger, penance, ritual atonement
ridding myself of reproach, all second guessing
I can't even think these words
Nothing has ever happened, all the time
in the world is here and gone and now

And then those promises I made arrive to remind me
they are relentless, I try not to attach to them
but I'm back at the Folsom Prison Writer's Workshop
remember Pancho, Gordon, Clyde, Willi X, Gerry Pena
remember the out of body feeling walking
through security and inside those stone walls
remember when you heard the news Gerry'd been killed
remember when the loudspeaker gave the lockdown
you walked the wrong way with the prisoners
and they laughed told me go the other way
"Go back, you don't want to come this way, andy man"
remember the rifles trained on every gesture
and those massive walls & clanging iron doors
some of these men had done horrible things
some were framed, never had a chance
some testify they are political prisoners
some are twisted evil fucks
some want to live good & prosperous lives
some say they are victims of bigotry
some work at appearing rehabbed
some are saintly
most come from poor families
most can't identify with the dominant culture
one said to me the world is a prison
you just live in minimum security is all
you're just a trustee
One says Kant was right we cannot know
God Justice Immortality or Freedom
One says Custer put me here, Custer
and Fremont and Union Pacific
One says Cortez sent me down this road

and Pizzaro and Coronado
One says it was the Czar and Standard Oil
and JP Morgan and the Ku Klux Klan
One says it's the Pope built Folsom
the Pope and all who hate sex
One says what killed the Old Ways
killed the beauty in them
One says he put himself here
One says it was Santa Claus, yes,
they should have never told him Santa
was real because he never came to his house
One says who gives a shit
One says it's the snitch in everyone
Some are very sorry and some are not

In 1970 Allen Ginsberg sat at the ancient organ
in the house and solemnly sang Bill Blake:
"Can I see another's woe
and not be in sorrow too?"
I asked him "Do you think it's good to bum out
over other peoples' bummers? Will it help
if I am in sorrow too? I want to help. Look
at my beautiful boy baby. Should he also be
in sorrow? What do you think about partying
as a cure for the sorrow of others?"
I was serious, and a pain in the neck
I'd been in Canada for nearly a year
I didn't know I was a pain
I thought I was a genius poet crusader
and I wanted a beautiful planet
for little Cassidy to grow up in.

I had fallen in love with ordinary folk
I proclaimed nuts & bolts as important
as etymology or calculus
I said laughter is prayer
and someone reminded how cruel
laughter can be
I said orgasm is revolution
and someone said yeah tell the kids
in Biafra they need orgasm
I said history never repeats itself
and someone said tell that to Mother India
I said it's all supernatural
and someone said murder war deceit money
brutality
that someone said any sick square
can learn nuts & bolts
any selfish brat can learn etymology
most any woman can bear a child
Stalin had a hearty laugh, a salt
of the earth laugh
Hitler loved dogs & children
was a vegetarian
Nixon slaps his knee hee haw
Bob Hope & his bevy of bathing beauties
makes thousands of GIs shout for joy
while the bombs fall on Cambodia
Pinochet Somoza Pol Pot
they all laugh & party hearty
Someone asks me do I really believe
all this grief is due to us not getting our nut?
Was Reich correct are we criminally
repressed in our loins?

Are the Hollywoodian aging Howdy Doody faced
leaders haunted by their sexual misery?
Someone tells me patriarchy is the tractor
of private property
I look out at the horizon
and marvel at the guy I was 12 years ago
then and now I need enlightenment
I need some answers
I don't want to be a pain anymore
        pain anymore
        pain anymore
            pain anymore
              pain.

Cherry Valley, NY, 1982, recalling first visit, 1970

V

AUSTIN & DENVER & OAKLAND —
WORKING FAMILY LIFE

"To Labor is to Pray"
Old Latin Proverb, Frank Clausen, Jr. often recited.

"Before I'll be any man's slave
I'll be a rotting down in my grave
and you can bury me in my dirty over alls."
Woody Guthrie, "Dirty Over Alls"

"You will eat by and by
In that glorious land above the sky
Work and pray, live on hay
and you'll get pie in the sky when you die."
Josef Hillstrom, "Pie in the Sky"

To my Children & their Mother
You are the Best
I wasn't
You Are

GUTENBERG'S BIBLE

Blake's Infant's Joy
Poe's printer ready impeccable hand
Whitman's deles & stets & stanza juggling
behind glass, even I a commoner can see
      for free at the University of Texas

I want to turn the page on Blake's "Song of Innocence"
      but, no, it's old & delicate
      and if we all could peruse these manuscripts
      at will, the originals would soon cease to exist
I've the feeling that most of these know little of Whitman
"I Hear America Singing," "Captain, My Captain," maybe
      a couple more. *Democratic Vistas,* a long shot.
      Certainly few of these know about Pete Doyle
      or Ann Gilchrist or the famous letter from
      Emerson or his job as nurse during the Civil War
Blake, probably "Tyger, Tyger." Gutenberg, they know
      the Bible cost 2 million, so that's big. Poe
      sure that's the author of *The Raven.*
Point being they look at but read not a word.
I feel they are here because it's the cultural
      thing to do

Later in the day I'm with my viper buddies
Today they are getting drunk for no woman's sakes
bitching & griping about how money is & isn't
talk motors & tools, brag about being foolish
come up with the best excuses for getting smashed
the walls are flying around, the floor is dancing
the charleston the shimmy the pony the locomotion
a playboy centerfold's passed around, each makes
a remark like: yeah. Then color photos of a new
model 4 wheel drive and the reactions about the
same as for the centerfold nice stuff they can't
have, when I mention this and that I care more
about the original Blake & Whitman mannys than the
playmate & vehicle they say it's lucky I
brought a six pack.

Austin, Texas 1980

ISOTOPIC MISERY

I've got isotopic miseries
I've got the ideoblastic blues
I've got the contradictory mulligrubs
I've got the isotropic funk
I'm searching the *Rocky Mountain News*
        for the Muse's personal message
A message from solar plexus to brain
        down the arm into hand and out
        my tool a remedy, not a remission
        but a cure
Doesn't have to be extasy
        just a little joy waking up
        to an ordinary morning
Not just a vacation
        but a different job
Not sleeping in late
        but aerobic passion & valor
Not a spoonful of sugar
        but unlimited uterine milk
The little obscure sect of the readers
        of verse don't want descriptions
        of dirty table cloths in their poetry
Nor inexplicable inextricable labrynthian

      whinings of me against the literary
      establishment
Nor the unsaid resentment of the wife
      peeling potatoes as the husband
      swills dissatisfaction with who he is
      in the minds of his peers
      the impotency he feels on the street
      at home in bed
No this is not what the lovers of verse want
They don't want advertising products
      other media handle with unbelievable
      results
They don't want hype about someone's new
      found religious can't miss ritual
They don't want hundreds of brand names
      all too familiar

They want Shangra La sung so fine
They want to taste Mt. Tokay's
      volcano nurtured wine
They want happy tears
They want to swim in Walden Pond
They want to sleep by Waterfalls
      deep & long
They want the vastness the wisdom
      of the silent roar of the Mojave
They want scenes not corrupted
      by greed
They want streets safe from danger
That's what the readers of verse
      want O Muse
They don't want the everyday misery

They want relief
They want escape
I can't blame them
So do I so do I
They want the Garden
          not the Sin
Can you deliver?
Reality's no priority
Realism is only another ism
Don't tell it like it is
          nor like it was or will be
Tell it like they want it to be
Don't you think they deserve it
Use me!

Boulder, 1980

INSTRUCTIONS FOR THE POETRY TAX COLLECTOR

Let them count the flaps of the not yet extinct
    Peregrine Falcon's getaway
Let them count the chews of Cambodian orphans
    on a dead guerilla's meager ration
Let them count the steps of the waitress
Let them scansion her tired wired fired hired footage
Let them mark the steps of chosen perfect youth
    to the old fool's altar of sacrifice
Let them mark the tracks of the human animal
    looking for work in the depressed city
Let all bow knowing they must bow like an oft
    conquered esne to the Lord of All
    the RENT
Let them put a meter on my bed
Let them count the worms of the dead
Let them rhyme everything that's said
Let them count mouths & bites of bread
Let them do it to every book they've read
Let them assay the amount every soldier bled
Let them audit the tax I paid in my head

Denver, 1980

108

CORNBALL

Supporting one's family by destroying
        what one loves i.e. the land
the open spaces that remain
the watershed, wildlife, the sky
        the ionosphere
I'm told by pragmatic buddies, my parents,
        & strangers, these feelings of regret
           are corny useless
I got to do what I got to do
A man's got to do what a man's got to do
        and aren't I a man?
I should be thankful I'm not on the dole
I should be damn grateful I'm not part
        of those desperate legions
        kept in check by borderline rations

I'm a cornball wanting some life that exists
        only in a painting
I'm a sap with a vericose mind desiring
        some edenesque life on the cover
        of *Watchtower*
I'm like those redundant deluded old geezers
        pining for impossibly glorified old days

I'm like some 1970's Native American who really
        thinks this continent will go back
                to the Old Ways
I'm like some Afro-American doing time
        dreaming of a pristine noble
                pre-colonial life in Zaire
I'm like some Chicano who thinks the Aztecs
        are going to make a comeback
I'm a wet eyed Walt Whitman type; I won't
        see the tirelessness of frontier cruelty
nor the tolerance of bigotry that which I named
The Mother of a Good and Equal Brood was capable of
        until old age
I'm a bright eyed frenchman who thinks
        the Revolution will usher in the Millennium
But the landlord has brought me back to earth
        the concrete & asphalt covered earth
So I do not put my one pair of sabot in the gears
I distill & drink my tears, before they're shed, instead
        crawling through the mud for a dollar
being a man, doing what a man's got to do

                    sometime in the 70's, probably Calif.

FAILURE

I'm paranoid of failure
My successes seem like failure
when I look out the window
When one's broke the money
of the past is failure
When folk speak of one's future
they mean money
They mean children who will not fail
Stalin made Lenin a failure
Kronstadt made Trotsky a failure
A liver blown beaten Indian in an alley
An evicted family living out of a car
An asbestos dying never missed a day
A man of God preaching racism
A forest destroyed for toilet paper
A war fought for interest rates
A government built on stealth
This ego craving thing power
This brutality to the environment
This religion as big business
guarantees failure
This demeaning of working with hands
This demand for ass kissing loyalty

This faith in firepower
paints an eternal winter of pathetic failure
The Birch tree knows it's been raining
The Holly tree knows it too
I'm stuck in the same job
and my songs of the open road
of being a rambler & a gambler
are less than fantasy, they're sick
I really dreamed I could make a difference
that I could take over where the others
left off, that I could make the dead champions
of justice freedom the poor the planet
successes. I mean who, who did I think
I was?—— no, no, I'm not Jesus Christ
I'm just another failure

Berkeley, 1978

TESTICLES

My buddy, who's an ambitious genius, objects
    to my using the word testicles
    instead of just saying balls
    like regular people do
He says penis doesn't cut it either
What self respecting fellah says penis?
    it sounds so dirty, so clinical
He says nuts, jewels, even gonads
    beats the austere testicles
So I make a non clinical list to replace penis:
    hoe, hammer, tool, pipe, third leg, ralph
    duke, champ, cock, satan, pecker, gun
This is my rifle, this is my gun
This one's for shooting, this one's for fun
That's how they taught us the difference
    in the Corps
I had a girl friend who called it parajito
    little bird, when she said it, it was okay
I admit penis has a penned in sound like penal
    but doesn't testicle sound religious
    serious upstanding, yeah I know that's
    where testimony came from because before
    the Bible a man would hold his testicles

to attest to his veracity
The penis dick whatever is a strange creature
    sometimes seems to have a mind of its own
It's a trouble maker for sure
O I know some call it the second mind
Others call it the Other
The Other & His Testicles
The ruin & rue of many a young man's dreams
It's kind of like a rose
no matter what you call it, it's still a rose
Naming it is not the problem

Oakland, 1978

ROSALEE

Depression born burnt out rural white gal
       with thick glasses and sad skin
waits tables at the Slow Poison Cafe
The other waitresses make fun of her
       behind her back
She has a tough time writing her orders
       properly but tries real hard
Her ulcer's getting worse
       she's been tired a long time

Rosalee once had a dream
Yeah, she had a dream, a small dream
Queen of the Honky Tonk
A woman old boys drank with & wanted
She rode with the rhinestone messiah
She rode with him in the ambulance
She rode with a guy named Hank
       to the Ford plant
She rode with the Cherokee Cowboy Band
yeah, rode with Harry the never finds
       work refrigerator man
Rode with Boxcar Slim & Mr. Next Time
       No good Dean the Rounder
Vito a fast talking Italian Jew
       from a place pronounced Wooster
Yeah she had a dream, old Rosalee

instant mud, newspapers she can hardly read
        cigarettes she can hardly quit
smoke traveling through hoops she can
        no longer jump through
a carousel with an off key calliope
        helps the gin go down
eyes closed welcomed by her only friend
        this sunday morn
her 5th hand butt burned burgundy chesterfield

the other waitresses can't imagine at one time
        Rosalee would quit a job for fun
She'd quit a job because the sun shined
        on an Okie holiday
She'd quit to go skinny dipping
        with a cute drifting pearl diver
The others don't know she can't remember
        her childhood or the day she lost
        the man she loved more than anything
The radio's crooning divorce, cheating, booze

Yesterday she changed her own flat tire
Yesterday her cheap shoes made her corns
        scream
Yesterday she walked plenty
Rosalee's mother's been dead long time
Rosalee never gave live birth
        and it's mother's day
Rosalee was made to smile at butterflies
She was made for apple pie picking
Made to make love under the tree
Made for watermelon on sundown porches

Not for vericose hells & hysterectomy
Not aspirins by the handful
not mother's day with a bottle & the radio
Her laugh made many a good man laugh
She wore them jeans ate them beans
drank from the bottle with the lost boys
slept next door to the used up hookers
and she swore *that* she wouldn't do
and then she met Jim and she wanted
     a home with him
she'd be his queen and he was sick so much
     she won the bread & took care of Jim
she took the orders & cook's abuse
Had her ass pinched by pigs in cotton shirts
with breath as foul as their words
She swallowed her own words for
     the paycheck & for Jim
And one day he was gone with a girl
friend she brought home

Rosalee baking cornbread & riding horses
     changing your water pump
strumming your five and dime guitar
putting on a non put on smile
You don't belong here sitting at home
     sleeping without dreams
after the crying
     on mother's day
       Rosalee

Oakland, 1976

DOGSHIT

My friend says insurance companies stole his job
He says the penal system makes criminals!
He says headlines are brainwashing tools!
He says headline writers are secret police!
He says all organized religions deceive
He says the industrial revolution is collapsing

I want to understand where he gets this stuff
How do you arrive at these conclusions?
He says by weeping tears of yellow rain
        by remembering the faces
        by the anger you feel standing in line
        by the insincerity of whores
I say I understand your passion but I don't
        know what you're driving at
He says don't you know? Democracy is mugged
        before the cameras
        the human sunflowers are etiolated
        fed dog shit
Man, don't you know the voters don't have a vote?
        despair can't be washed out of pubic hair
I say what have you been smoking?
He says, man, don't be so naive

Don't you know apples & pears are not what they seem?
Don't you know they sell God to the highest bidder?
Haven't you heard of the Golden Nimrod?
Don't you know all the reactors will melt?
Don't you know the Russians build nukes
          with used parts?
Don't you know they make senators lick
          the armpits of oil companies?

I said wait a second slow down I want to get this
          right, what was that about selling God?
He says God eats dog shit!
I said don't say that
He said it doesn't matter
He says it's really Mary Magdalene who's hung
          on the cross and God is dog shit!
I said Jesus how can you say that?
He says God's everywhere right?
He says the church is shit, the tabernacle shit!
He says muff diving is a sacrament
He says original sin is beauty
The greatest thing man has done is eat
          the forbidden fruit!
That the meek inherit only 6 feet of earth
He says Adam & Eve knew nothing about God
He says Jesus came to destroy the old testament
He says fucking & sucking is how we worship God
He says I have to understand everything he says
          or I will spend Eternity in Hell!

Oakland, 1976

Like I Could Get You Out

the brother is auditioning to fill the vacancy
      in the writer's workshop
"Someone got stabbed in Folsom Prison today
He had a mother had a father a brother"

in the library I can see out the open door
      the yard so small for so many men
I can't shake those eyes
Somewhere sometime we rode together
I know you, You know me, your eyes hold mine
      like I could something — like I knew —
      like I could get you out

and there's trouble in the yard
      an excruciating buzzer sounds & everyone freezes
outside I see the combatants fighting with every limb
      shivs shining in the Repressa sun and a squadron
      of former linemen in full riot gear double time
      in to kick booty like robots as everyone's still
      rifles trained up in the towers

Folsom Prison, 1975

THEY ARE COMING

There are many historical male poet derelicts
but the women all beautiful or well to do
         save the obscure few
but when the derelict women
         come for the laurel wreath
when the hag haired sots smile
         thru rotting mouths with atrophied wombs
eructating abortions & other misfortunes
this scene will change

They'll come from food stamp streets
         like everything wrong television
they won't need know the Clorox
         test for cocaine
or what myriad undulations of liberation
mean to co-eds masturbating at Bergman movies
they'll come with tired feet
         of concrete floors canneries & beaneries
they'll come with bleached eyes & blue lips
they'll come from lost children memories
         and pimped gone beauty
they'll come with dignity
they'll come like Mothers
The derelict women poets are coming!

Oakland, 1975

121

OOMBA

On schedule wake one minute before alarm
every morning one minute before
now that's alarming
this morning was just about to receive
a jail sentence and I swear I was
like the Nazarene before Pilate
what is this about?
roll over listen buzzing
not intended to be pretty
get a little
two rubbers broke
got 3 kids, that's enough
O well 45 seconds of bliss
AM radio for AM
traffic dexedrine djs
breakfast reheat bulgur
think it's not russia
instant mud from 7–11 score
almost clean work trousers
through the machine twice
shoes shirt socks get them
on in proper order
cement decorated hat
keys glasses sandwich

late, thermos
please don't break it
like the last dozen or so
kiss.
behind.
fire up
two ways
hell ten ways
rear view clear
got oil got water got gas
sound
new junk yard solenoid
stop sign, check with eyes
in face ontop neck
here comes new paint pick up
avoid, bad clutch work
car exhales in unison wit' me
ramp ram up ram ram freeway
here comes Contra Costa to Frisco
bridge backup rush
intimidating crazy jacked
chew tobacco
guts guts ball on in out
call on deep self
no surrender self
tears why tears
how this happen to me
I'm 12 years old
I'm gonna play for the New York Yankees
I'm gonna be a big time beatnik poet
elevator on outside of building
crew's on the way up

I'm late, slam park
grab run 4 minutes late
runup 11th floor stairs
Jack reminds me I'm late
wheel barrow
concrete scraper, concrete breaker
broom room rooms shovel hunh!
loins still sticky
tobacco juice bad coffee mex reg jay
first thrust my shoulder small of back
inside my shoes what I've been doing
what I do 8 hours a day hunh!
time after time hunh!
most people most normal people
have no idea what this is about
most people most normal people
wouldn't do this for love or money
and that's exactly why I do it
love and money hunh!
I think this is the sentence
the judge was going to give me
and my crime is karma
and my time is after time
and that's what I'm doing hunh!
unh! Hunnh! clang sting spark
rang ring thud dead mud oomba hunnh!
unnh hunnh hooo uunnh wham slam bing
unnh wooah hunnh! huunnh! hunnh!
OOmba!

Oakland, 1975

ALL THIS PAINTING IS TALKING ABOUT

He's giving me advice: Study feet to learn beauty
Who is it gives advice like that?
Well he's a terrific under-recognized painter
His next tidbit: Shine your eyes on the coats
        of masterless dogs
He says look deep into his paintings
        and write the first thoughts in my mind
I said the first thoughts or first words?
He says just do it

Here goes: Bless this cup of go on say the unfulfilled
        closing saturday nite sounds dis-nerving St. Francis
        birds of challenge on your shoulder
A good drummer who'll show up is hard to find
This one coughs vomit, dry heaves days
        of endless nights dragged like defeated
                mexican bulls gurgling paint
                on the flies of dust
                down in the arena of lust without love
        raining rose petals & tragic boredom

He says that's good don't stop now
Here goes again: The magnificent pachuco Lorca

posts up outside the Red Irish Oakland bar
down in the land of store bought tortillas
broken cars, broken friendships, broken hearts
broken families, windows, teeth, treaties
karma is after the fact
The Human Be-In
this pulsating tapestry
clean mind golden birds sleeping in green dolphin
rooms singing piney atmospheric sparks of prajna
All this painting is talking about is the movie
lived in the text of the sky talking to deep
winter hooks in our eyes married
to this canvass destroying our emotional
response to Life after Death
the second chance we easily refused
driving love away from her body
the model & inspiration of all this color
& extravagance in our not empty long glasses
toasting our new unanswerable art
something even a baby could understand:
She's gone. Man, she is gone.

Berkeley, 1975

VI

SAN JOSE, BERKELEY — THE 60'S GONE — THE NIXON YEARS

"Be-Bop is an attitude."
Bill Young

"The Hippie is dead. Money's the new Acid."
Popular saying of early 70's in San Jose

"My man is eaten by the gonorrhea of war
My Poem will be building in the blood of
young men
and I shall remember what they have been
forced to forget"
Kenneth Patchen, "The Hunted City"

To the Gone, Bill Young, Be-Bopper,
Master of the Traps, Painter, saint of goof

HALFWAY

They are called among other things, halfways
        cause they live in halfway houses
Pity adds to sorrow
Pity is not love
It's not that much better
than hate, revenge or misery
the fools I've known weren't always foolish
the wisemen weren't always wise
the crazies weren't always crazy
        etcet
But a halfway is supposed to be halfway
        to functioning in society
I see them out my window standing on the sidewalk
        just standing there, thorazine I guess
Slow Boat to China spins on the HiFi

These guys ought to be working on a mural
Who was it said everybody's an artist?
These guys ought to be given a ration of pot
They should stand on the seashore
They should look for interesting seaweed
They should gather driftwood for sculpture
They should do about anything other
        than just standing on that sidewalk
waiting for someone who'll never show up
staring at me staring at them

San Jose, 1974

BE-BOP = ATTITUDE

Driving through the gauntlet of stucco apartments
Driving through the smell of burning gasoline
    the smell of fast food
Mechanical sound all around a kind of insanity
    contagion that has driven many over
    edge of flat world
I proclaimed Be-Bop the suppressed act
    of overpriced free enterprise
Can there be a medicine that makes oppression
    not tolerable yet less hurtful?
Yes, music to literally move people
    fun for the intellect
    a work out & massage — a grace
    hip to the otherside of the moon
    an honorable reprieve?
An attitude the recordings can't quite capture
    unstoppable Zonga drenched chords
    inside out at supersonic speed of seed
The great African after-beat & kinetics
        have sex with the Age of Enlightenment
The unceasing true escape
The go will be gone call & response
The flaming french horn outer space campfires

The second avenue gotham taxi assiduous brushes
The weed in the sidewalk crack dignity solo
The folk songs of 10,000 human years
        translated by the orchestra
        from Mars arranged outside in
The Georgia pine shack sprung shackles
        rattling down the main line
        smokestack on wheels of
        oscilating boogie-ing conception
        like Tibetan horns & bells
        at a downtown pace of the chase
        that haunts every coping face
        and exhales musical neologism
What is the opposite of Be-bop?
Is it opposition to the pleasures of the Bod?
Is it beauty made ugly by won't quit redundancy?
Is it a tyrannical boredom that states the problem
        as too much freedom?
Define Be-Bop, the cronies demand
and I repeat the meaning, a man was Be-Bop,
hipped me to, yes, Be-Bop is an Attitude

San Jose, 1974

THE SPOILS OF WAR

A man inside a house he has to tolerate
night after night after night
A woman working working working
six nights a week
She leaves at four and he takes over
taking care of the kids
Outdoors is just a place to make money
which takes care of what they need
to make money
making love in the morning
and on with the levis & boots
he's out the door and it's her
turn to watch the kids
They hadn't paid attention to the trends
and thought kids was the thing to do

Television more than a babysitter
becomes a surrogate parent
He thought it's too bad we aren't farmers
He thought this isn't the way
Hurried and tired sex as a link to sanity
The physical damage to their nerves, lungs
heart hands backs minds self esteem

The microwave oven will be big
under these conditions
The headlines will run amok
and soon he'll be dead to their violence
heartbreak & doom
If coffee were illegal he'd be an outlaw
If it wasn't for self medication he'd do him-
self in, he needed a dream silencer
This is not the America he'd learned about
in Civics class, this is not the one
he saw on the silver screen
She was a hard working loving devoted
wonder woman and yet their lives
were steeped in frustration
Pioneers, a new breed, of both parents
working can't get aheads
World War II's spoils were losing clout
            losing meaning losing US

San Jose, 1973

THE GARBAGE FED TOMS SCREECH

the garbage fed toms screech
big trucks gear down at red lights
exhaust & litter dervish
concrete & asphalt condom
the composting sex of nature
reading faces between the lines
reveals the have or not of money
some of the younger have nots
have fight written all over them
the sky is smeared with human excretion
this liquor store is a rough one
a loud siren curbs the traffic
eyes filled with blood demand coins
and if unsuccessful plead
"I'm gonna get sick, young bro,
36 cents, I need 36 cents"
these eyes project disdain, impatience,
get pissed off
One feels these would be a mugger's eyes
if they weren't so sick
His tongue is bright green
probably drank a bottle of Nytol

There's dog shit everywhere
The boosters try to look nonchalant
A silk tropical shirt clad pimp
dodges the dog shit in his eye-talians
So does the hard faced off duty whore
in her platforms going to cop
my old buddies find me here
want me to go to a party
with them in another neighborhood
where they drink Mateus & Blue Nun
not Gallo Tokay, Arriba, Silver Satin
at the party they have real opium
and lovely girls with perfect teeth
and guys with permawave locks
& Martin guitars & new cars
All the black people are
in the record cabinet
I hate what I write
what I try to pass off as poetry
My teeth hurt & look gross
I've been sleeping 15 hours a day
At night I chant loaded mantras
Hare mama Hare dada
mama mama dada dada
and after running out of steam & gas
pray with my entire being
that UFOs come & take me

Berkeley & Orinda, 1973

Seeking A Fool Proof Riff

I'm walking around looking for a fool proof riff
some notes or words I can call on & won't be failed
Some mantra or hum make this foray into North Beach
        special
Motor oil burning rubber & fish, linguinis, garlics
        sourdough, sherry, pork entrails, steam grease
        sweat, metallic dust, seaweed, chilis, perfumes
Bubble gum colored neon girlies, light bulb nipples
Sidewalk barkers "take a look"
A hooker with a nasty shiner, fat lip
Yes I contend to administer energy to seduce
        only love from your face like Job
Eric Dolphy's flute doing Feathers for Bird
        inspire this verse!
Sound of the ground neath the concrete
        inspire the feet of me!
Let the sky filled with Miles inspire this!
Let the faith that I keep be the beat!
Man living off garbage cans inspire me
Artists ejaculating no substance goad me
The Big Avocado, I follow the coffee O inspire
Bob Seider playing How High the Moon
        in the closed bank entrance turn me on!

Bob Kaufman in a Dashiki with a lexicon
        of only phonemes caging beers, yes!
Paddy O'Sullivan gruffly reciting
           like a Bluebeard flowery verse
           to the sidewalk unmassed masses
           give me strength!
Eileen Kaufman winking twitching & smiling
           in the Trieste with young friends
           teach me by osmosis
The guy at Gino & Carlos who sings
           up we go into the wild blue yonder
           I should be so bold!
Allen & Peter at Shigs
           giving advice to forget bitterness
           towards the poetry powers, temper me.
Paul Vane & Carol Lee Sanchez make it live
Ntozake Shange with colored beads in her hair
           dancing her poems about saxophones
             & abuse, hip me
A woman I met at the Kerista house
           who took me to the Hell's Angel Ball
           where Janis & Big Brother were the band
           remember me
Handsome so at ease horn player with beret who advised
           me not to chase women "let them come to you"
           I will live like I believe you!
The tall well intentioned communist meter perfect
           over socialised bleeder, make me sigh
The indian who says he's FBI, full blooded indian
           who says Indians discovered Columbus
           give me laugh & pause & strength to never forget
Woman all in blue point me to the true how do you do

The mumbler who's doing it for free brew
        give me laugh & pause
The woman with the long cigarette holder
        & gown reciting surrealistic empathy
        for the proletariat, all of you
        inspire me to sign the open poetry list

San Francisco, 1972, Coffee Gallery

START THE SUN

My son's just started talking
He shouts "Start the sun! Start the sun!"
This makes me proud, he's a natural poet!
Linda's brewing a fresh pot of coffee
It's a typical foggy grey bay summer day
I can hear cars sucking wind
their wheels making industrial music
       on the tone deaf street
The truck gears sound like hungry monsters
Airborne ships of state sonic boom
The paper says powers that be are contemplating
towing ice bergs to LA
Many are dying right now, many dying broke
many are plotting assinations without fear
the real killers of JFK, Malcolm, Martin, Bobby
       they'll never spend a day in jail
doors are being broken down because folk smoke gage
officials who smash heads & kick the defenseless
       are heroes to the powers that be
       just as long as it's the right heads smashed
"Start the sun!" my boy commands again.
The air traffic reminds me of the war in Nam
Even though I haven't read a paper or listened

to radio or TV in 5 months
I know the war in Nam is still happening
The 3 year old doesn't know
He wasn't told the spirit of the bayonet is to kill
He wasn't told the enemy is called gook
He wasn't told napalm is 9 times hotter than fire
        and sticks to the skin therefore
        a wonderful invention
He doesn't know thousands maybe millions will die
        because of something called the domino theory
He just knows someone should start the sun!

Later in the day I tell my buddy Al how my 3 year old
        yells start the sun! and yet I can't help but
        start everyday thinking about that war in Viet
        Nam
Al says, "Why be concerned with our 51st state?"
        expecting a laugh I presume.
I can't, I can't laugh, and that's bad.
I want a world, a nation, a humanity worthy
        of my beautiful son
So start the sun, godamnit, start the mother fucker
        up!

Berk, CA, 1972

DIABLO

Diablo, one of ten, from melon town to cotton town
          they'd ask where you been?
knew the pain of abusive work in his back & hands
          by the time he was eight
youth blurred by sweating dust and cheap wine
          in the hot valley sun
Diablo knew being hungry mornings & nights
          knew jail, knew the couldcareless hustlers
            knew degradation, knew hard & easy ways
fixed rides with bailing wire, fashioned parts
          from scraps, boosted tools, hot wired
tequila codeine, milking not burning down friends,
stuff in the arm, filling up his nose
dice, cards, ponies, laughed in the hit man's face
was like a movie Small Timer defies the Big Boys

Diablo put the hurt on a famous gunsel
          with more than fist
Did county time where others like him
          watched his back
Diablo hit the iron, the books, made money
          came out singing Praise the Lord
            had women believing he was Christ
Played bongos while the city slept
          had religious sex behind coke
          had wild sex & bread behind belief
Then one night he saw the ghost of Joaquin Murrieta
          take the shotgun seat and speak to him

Joaquin wanted Diablo to have a purpose
Joaquin had watched Diablo for awhile
Joaquin convinced him to be a revolutionary
Diablo would be like an escaped stallion
　　　　returning at night to coax others
　　　　to join him in escape
Corridos were made about him
Blues were built around his legend
He rode low in his ride
He'd go to where women couldn't sleep
　　　　cantinas, fields, corners, dance halls
Diablo was recruiting
Diablo preached hatred of Anglo laws
His main towns were Stockton Tracy Hayward
　　　　Oakland Modesto Fresno San Jose Seattle
Soon the uprising would begin
and Murrietta would ride again

One day a rejected woman called the heat on Diablo
She had lost her mind and an hour after calling
　　　　she put her head in an oven
　　　　but the gas had been turned off the day before
Diablo had been dealing smack
　　　　and buying weapons
California would again belong to Californians
Six cops surround him in Mariella's front room
outside even more police
Diablo was smoking marijuana dreaming a movie
　　　　based on a book about the life of Che Guevara
He was half way through, and had drifted away
　　　　from the text envisioning his speech
　　　　to his people that life was going to change

they would no longer work like animals
would no longer be humiliated, would now
share in the bounty
He takes a toke, puts the roach in the ashtray
and stands up his hands out to be cuffed
The cop's handcuffs rattled, their drawn pieces
shaking
The house was searched, a little skag was found
He was dragged outside by the cuffs
shouting to the neighborhood he's bailed out
manyana or the one who did this is no more

impossible bail was set
the woman who ratted overdosed on heroin
The Law hangs Diablo from the ceiling
a couple of his high school adversaries
now cops with big bellies beat him
with rubber hoses
they want the location of his arsenal

Joaquin tells Diablo not a word
Diablo gets the maximum sentence
He is denied parole again & again
He resists joining a tip, a prison gang
no one messes with him
He repels hired aryan assassination
He preaches his own interpretation of marxism

One day he'll walk the streets again
He'll be an old man
He'll ask you a question

Felton, California, 1972

CALL IT BLUES

call it bad medicine
call it months without sun
call it a job you hate & hate
call it a marriage on the run
call it 99 kinds of mean
call it the kiss of gethsemane
call it going down on golgotha avenue
but you can't call it anything new

I hear people talking about kindness
don't even know what it means
I hear them debate mercy all night
while we fight for rice & beans
there's no white washing
a house burnt by the blues
there aint no talkin alone
fix a house made of bad news

call it lethal emanations
call it artificial scarcity
call it cruel mockery
call it a sad call from jail
call it one who tried died wrong
call it grief without relief
call it a drink you must refuse
call it eaten alive by the blues

(repeat chorus)

Eugene, Oregon, 1971

LENNY

Lenny ahead of his thoughts
like an electrically shocked cartoon
a marionette manipulated by spasm
and somehow its body language
shouts love me love me just love
cranked like the assembly line
in Chaplin's *Modern Times*
like Charlie dodging bullets
during the prison break scene
the words spewing out of control
as he analyzes himself
on his back on the stage
coaxing himself to get up, Lenny,
and do your gig, the narcs the feds
the powers that be want Lenny gone
his life in shreds and the crowd
laughing thinking it's a schtick
no one will rescue him Lenny knew it
but Lenny wouldn't quit
the great comedian is not funny
the clown's make-up runs
the audience hides, friends hide
doctors pull Pontius Pilates out of hats
Caiphas, Hoover, the legions of Rome,
the legions of indecency, the gestapo,
joe friday, the hypocrites, the vultures,
the maggots, the south east north & west
there's no direction for Lenny to go
after up & down are exhausted

all that's left is out
Yeah Lenny you were funny & smart
you were brilliant most always
interesting and relevant
but what I most admire is your guts
You didn't let them take you alive

(After seeing footage of Lenny's last
performances sometime in the seventie:
with a chill running up my spine
no horror flick could come close to
i can't be around that much crank
even if it's just a movie)

VII

OREGON & ALASKA & MONTANA & CANADA — UP COUNTRY

"The Earth is an Indian thing"
Jack Kerouac, Mexican Fellaheen
(Lonesome Traveler)

"It's just a dream, just a dream
Look you have nothing and neither do I
Save for having each other
and the choice of how we die
Damn it to hell, can you see any other solution
Here's to you old man, to you and the Revolution"
AC, "Here's to You Old Man"

In memory of John Edmonston
Backwoods Sage

SONG OF THE SISKIYOU

Blue steel glowing cold Siskiyous
The sidewindows framing magnificent postcards
My retinas: cameras filming what will delight
       the future audience in my future skull
What will thrill the pulsing in my future chest
The soundtrack Himalayan rumbling bass te deum
         obscure keyed jazz moving into Rockaway Blvd.
         be-bop contrapuntals expanding into gigantic
         ganglias of unearthly colored wheels of notes
raining over the driver side windshield cracked
       in shape of Crazy Horse's war paint
The lightening streak on left cheek

In Denver,
Bob Morehouse, Sioux hod-carrier, told me
Crazy Horse's name translated literally
       is Large Dog Crazy
Crazy's original name was Curly
Large Dog is what the Oglala Sioux
         called a horse when they first saw them
         and it stuck
America is the regendered first name
        of an Italian map maker

It could have been his last name Vespucci
We could be Vesputians
They weren't going to name it after an Indian
         person or idea

This is the California-Oregon border
My Hispanic surnamed buddy says it's Mexico
It's the land of the Siskiyou & Klamath
It's the land of brother bear
Can you hear mama bear growl?
Can you hear the Trickster howl?
The sky is scattered like notes of Bartok
I can't see nor smell any pollution
There's too much air for the carbon monoxide!
The only way I know it's the USA
         are those red white & blues lights
         that can pull me over anytime
         to remind me
This the great USA the one that will make
Krushchev's boast about burying it a laughing
         stock of history
This is the USA that above all rewards hard work
This is the USA that defines freedom
This is the USA that boasts we're No. One
This is the place that ironically calls itself
         The Home of the Brave
This is where I hear the Ghost Dancers
         in the wind
This is where I hear the sound
         of Chief Joseph's voice
         as it opts for peace
This is where I hear Santanta's defiant shout

      leaping off the mental hospital wall
This is where I hear the hand muzzled first cry
        of the Cheyenne baby on the exodus trail
          from Oklahoma concentration camp to Wyoming
          homelands, muzzled by mother so not to give
          away the fleeing tribe's position
          to ethnic cleansers
This is where I can hear the last 30,000 years
          in my old woodstove cranking up
             breathing like a locomotive
I hear the popcorn exploding on cold nights
I hear the brokenhearted yellow label jukeboxes
          loving em leaving em pining & whining
I hear the logging trucks spraying rain
          the choker chains, the chainsaws
I hear glass broken & fist fights
I hear what a broken treaty sounds like
I hear a jalopy run out of gas
I hear a sermon not on the mountain
          but from the Mountain
The earth shall inherit the meek
          & bold alike
O I know they say there's little future
          in the past
and everyone knows nothing only nothing lasts
but somewhy I keep hanging I keep hanging onto you
Immortal song of the Siskiyou

            I-5 going home to Blue River, 1970
               (Crazy Horse stanza, 1981)

LITTLE WALTER IN EUGENE

1970 I'm a loser back in Eugene
out of work, listening to Little Walter
"night time is falling
the pain is coming down again
you know people I aint got no friends"
next door the hippies are playing
somebody called sweet baby james
we're almost out of wood, it's cold
my shit hasn't been together for weeks
I go drink java in the redneck diner
they think I'm one of them
the bars around town have discovered
topless dancing
I went into one by accident
I never saw a sadder bunch of redneck
boys & businessmen in my life
the girls faces didn't look real
the men guilty as sin
back at the diner the chain smokers
are unaware someone put LSD in the water
How can they maintain?
I want to yell it's okay to freak out!
Instead I walk through the icy streets
back to the room and Little Walter

Ramona

She was born in a duplex tween railroad tracks
and interstate 5 when the wild blackberries
were overripe
17 days overdue by menstrual calculation
Lane county Oregon
We have her first scream on tape
Linda lay on a mattress clean sheeted
and padded with disinfectant ink of 1970's newspapers
wearing shades under the bright lights
of the overwhelmed camera man
who'd read the Encyclopedia Britannica
cover to cover but never
witnessed anything or nothing like this

Lottie, midwife we met on Halloween
her first solo, had assisted at 5—
14 people present, adults & children,
Beer, Chamomile tea, and the best childbirth
drug Indian Hemp
Loud hours, nervous humour hoped to calm
crazy me—
equipment ready
the space seperating contractions
condense at Malthusian speed

"Hold your breath, Linda" Lottie sez
I said "Pant like a dog"
our 18 month boy stopped asking questions
Linda had used the panting method
at his birth

She wrenched and arched her back
grimacing, holding my hand
(I'd told her "Go ahead & scream babe
I'll just slap my hand and shout
I tol' ya not to go out with Fred
and I aint gonner quit cigarettes neither
so, the neighbors'll think it's just another
country western fight")

She showed pain for O ninety seconds
the cervix expanded like you
don't expect to see a living thing
blood dripped over rose-like petals
of the opening
then visible brains corrugated
        like a dip chip or furrowed earth
a gasp in 13 bellies
a frightening humanness of Creation's Beauty
"Come on Babe"
I prayed to Life
A friend said "I see Hair!"
natural rubber gloves touched it
like a rabbit scooting under snow
it spit out
bright purple— "Is he the right color?"

"It's a she dummy" Mary informed me.
(I'd mistaken the umbilical cord between her legs
for a penis, but the sex perfect
we had no boy's name only girl's
Mona — Ramona)
but the color
no sound
for 9–10 seconds
then it came
it's on tape
a birthday present for her
for she turned towards pink slowly
wailing protesting the light
wrinkled a little head cheese couple
drops in the eyes, blue stained brown,
birth mark on neck shown
while weighed on bathroom scale
Linda's holding Ramona
Our eyes kiss our cheeks
Our lips touch our hearts
our minds fly with soul
laughing beers popping open
Lottie still too busy to drink hers
the Placenta had been stuck
I cut over to next door phone doctor
"Hi we've just had a birth and we'd like
to use the phone to call Dr. Rathbone,"
"Sure we thot somethin like that was going on.
Can I come over in a bit and see?"

Lottie pushed on belly like massage
gently tugged — out came a mass

of material unearthly
this Sustainment
The Tree of Life
like a piece of magic
science fiction beyond fiction
the richest of reds
the most iridescent grey

In the low ceiling room
we revel the minutes ago like world series victors
in the locker room
where no one lost
where we were all one team

Now all's safe
all joyous and up
the emptiness has brot a fullness
our daughter born into a great tribe
Ramona 6 1/2 to 7 lbs.
ten toes ten fingers, breath
one tooth, sucking Linda's breast
Chuck leaves his camera on the steps
a lid is strewn on the floor
Lover Wife Mother is beautiful with happiness
our son amazed wants a drink of water
friends are friends
Vitamin E applied externally

At midnight pink fluid from baby
normal — okay — sleep awake to rain
clean up beer bottles, ashtrays
dishes in sink and under

a strange neoprene bag with swishing
jello like matter
It's the placenta and tho some say
we should have ate it
at least buried it
and planted Roses
I just threw into garbage can with a thud
The sky was the color of the can
I hurried back inside.

Glenwood (Springfield), Oregon, November 1970

THE NIGHT I HEARD KEROUAC DIED

The night I heard he died
     I had to get outside
     even though it was a foul night
Ketchikan Alaska 48 inches of rain
     that October
I walked small steps
on the smooth wooden sidewalks
   like the ancient woman of ancient Cathay trucking on
     to face the void in the faces
     of clerks who've been brain snatched
     by extra terrestrial invaders
     ringing up my spuget & wine
without a word

The rain came in waves
I shouted: "Timber!"
moonless dark never enough money dark
The alcoholic salmon wail the cry of the sea wolf
The sawdust smoke of Ketchikan Spruce stank allright
The alchuringa Jack London left here
ornery & desperate — midst
     the misty medieval dungeon squeakings
     of the Green Chain — working till 2AM

Wharf rats they blame on Norway
        scurry about the forklifts
and wood skids

I buy the white haired air a drink
Here's to the last turn of the century
Here's to the Thlinket people
Here's to fish skin houses
Here's to sidewalks like wet driftwood
Here's to reading *On the Road* again
        at my 9 PM lunch
Here's to the fast colors & excitement
Here's to your adventures in a world
        no longer possible
Here's to you Jack, reading London & Wolfe
    & a world no longer possible

Here's to a best friend I never met
        a friend I touched
        a friend to talk to

I like the little lights of the little street
        in the driving wetness legging it home
the jukeboxes minus Lester Young
        blowing madness jubilee to
wide eyed jitterbug pilgrims
no pool hall mystics driving vehicles
        of Apocalyptic Sex
        ramming jamming nights ecstatic
        unkept rendezvous & hookey.

The sadness is no longer beautiful on the
        wino's face

It could have been your brother's father
I just have to smile and Bird plays
I just have to lid my eyes
          and Desolation Angels pass thru
I just have to pull on the bottle
          to receive your transmission
the Woody Woodpecker riff of Groovin High
Delivers Me
          Unreproaches Me!
takes the weight off! Shouts!
Timber! Jack! Jack Kerouac!
Timber!

(In Alaska, "Timber!" used to mean drinks are on me —
still might —of course also a tree falling)
                              Ketchikan, Alaska, 1969

GANDY DANCING MONTANA
(*THE DETERMINED PILGRIM*)

"Tamp em up boys, tampem up good
Good & firm, next joint! Ah!
forget it, take a break"

Pat Brady & I sat on the 93 degree
Milwaukee Road Rail for a break
the last major electric railway in the US
pick, short shovel, rails, ties, spikes,
mauls, tongs, jacks, gravel, snakes,
    flies like bumble bees
both pleasure & pain straightening up
    brains like leather
too tired to have egos

Down on the highway, I'd say a furlong
    and a half across the recently
    harvested alfalfa gainst the pine
    mountain background
A bent forward figure
    as if he were the focus of a great
    painting: *The Determined Pilgrim*
"Is that a nigger?"

161

the 19 year old summer job townie
    quarterback wants to know
"Yeah it is, it is!" confirms the 220 lbs.
blue eyed tackle going on to college ball
    (he can bench press 300)
The crew's idea of fun is to break beer bottles
    on girl's cars and hang moon
    or net a few hundred baby trout
    and watch them die in a 50 gallon drum

Pat & I watch their yelling insults & stones
    fall a football field short
"Fuckin nigger, fuckin boogie!"
Old John the section boss comments "the dirt
    is loose right here, we could bury him
    here, henh, henh, heh, heh" his
snickering reciprocated by all but Pat & I

John shouldn't have said that
He just thought it would endear him
    with the young ones
He shouldn't have said that
39 years on the railroad
He should be a leader of men.

If they weren't so tired
If it was another time
If the track was closer to the road
it could have been tar & feathers
they have the psyche for it
but he was a long way off
and there's been a civil rights act

for 5 years and the adrenaline
eventually sinks into them
I'm thinking "These poor blue balled
wretches."
I couldn't have dreamt back in California
I'd be working next to 19-20 year olds
as ignorant cruel & square as these miscreants
Their parents won no oscars with their
transparent hospitality
suspicious small minded uglies

We kept our picks sharp on the job
just sitting on the railroad tie
Pat asks me, "Andy what's going to become
of all these trees?"
Meaning the land was beautiful
but its inhabitants weren't
"It will take time" is what I said.
Both of us owed a lot to Afro-Americans

my truck had broken down here
and we were working our way out
I kinda liked one guy, 9 Mile
He'd the guts to sit next to us
got his name on account he lived
by the 9 mile marker
His brother was a bulldogger
and turned him onto speed
He drove 90 mph every chance he got
He had a stout red rubber "rodeo"
credit card he kept in the trunk
of his 53 Ford next to the flat spare

"I never take all their gas or from old
    can't afford it cars."
He said he was out as soon as he could do it
Maybe try bulldogging
I had a question for 9 Mile concerning
    The Determined Pilgrim
"Nine Mile you reckon that old boy (everybody's
    an old boy up here) will have to walk all
    the way to Superior?"
(a 24 mile distance)
"He'll walk the whole state."

Brady says, "He's probably from Chicago
    on his way to Seattle."

                  Alberton, Montana, July 1969

THESE ARE THE ONES

These are the ones, the poor, the laborering unaffected
        unsophisticated salt of the earth agonized ones
These are the people, Ma Joad's people, the blues
        singer's people, the backwoods & backalley ones
The ones who put one foot out at a time
        one day at a time & go on & on & on
These are the ones the wealthy artists can paint
        describe portray photograph
These are the people Whitman knew & believed in
These are the honest losers of the money game
The ones who share their last
    travel by bus & hitchhike & walk
These are the broken back shovelers, the black
        lunged menials, these are the fodder
The ones crucified next to the saviour
        the ones dumped into mass graves
These are the mothers who must read of son's
        death in foreign land

These are the ones computer society will leave behind
These are Blake's Sunflowers
Guthrie's One Great Big Soul
These are the people I love

The unglamourless ones
The mothers with too much work to do
The toddlers who don't know they're poor
The teenagers who know poverty too well
These are the children of sharecroppers
The ones who laugh in spite of all the bad
These are my chosen people

My love will give birth to our first any time now
And I like them nervously finger keys to an old
        wreck as if they were worry beads
I like them wait for my name to be called
Yes, these are the ones

Eugene, Oregon, 1968

TALKING DINNER TABLE

I tried to imitate my dad's dinner table laugh
A cynical reciting of the words *ho-ho-HO*
        and a little back hand wave & head turn
        and the laughter simulation was over
Dad didn't laugh much, right now I can't recall
        one instance of belly laugh
What I do remember is how he used to toss his burnt
        matches on his plate after dinner signaling
        it was okay to talk
sipping his Manhattan or strate Old Crow shrinking
        his brow his eyes on the spot where the wall
        met the ceiling scheming or contemplating
        whatever he had in his mind when he'd drag
        & puff on his filterless Camel and look
        like he'd come to a decision as heavy as
        the world.
Our mom would remind us dad was a "Good Provider."
When the matches hit the plate, we could talk.

Nashville, 1968

VIII

THE EARLY DAYS — PSYCHEDELPHIA & LEAVING MARINES

"He's the Universal Soldier and he really is to blame
His orders come from far away no more
They come from him and you and me
and brother can't you see
This is not the way we put an end to war."
              Buffy St. Marie, "The Universal Soldier"

"Know that today there are millions of Americans
seeking America... know that even with all
those eye-expanding chemicals--only more of
what is not there do they see."
              Gregory Corso, "Elegiac Feelings American"

To the Love Generation
Peaceniks & Protesters & Explorers of Inner Space
You weren't wrong

OIL CHANGE IN CICERO

I knew it was a sign
the world our culture
was changing, changing fast
fast as jet propulsion
and proverbial new york minutes
getting the oil changed
on the way out of Chicago
The station manager's a pork
bellied trash rappin cracker
His teenage employee's got
the Rolling Stones on the radio
"Get rid a that jungle bunny music
or turn it off!"
The kid's astonished, "But that's
the Rolling Stones!"
"I don't give a slimey slick shit,
let em come to Cicero, them burr heads
will get theirs! We know how to
deal with them round here. Change it!"
The kid changes the station
to Porter Wagoner like he's done it
a thousand times. The look he gives me
says something.

Cicero, Illinois, 1968

171

I LOOKED IN JERRY RUBIN'S EYES

He had a kerchief around his head
& a red flag in his hand
I said "Don't fight"
He looked at me as if I were vermin
I checked out the cops, they wanted
to use their billy clubs
their eyes charged with bad intentions
We had a baby in the mixer
We had to get out of there

One large room with bath second floor
One week the water was brown
It wasn't a hallucination
It came out the tap
The papers said we could try to wash
with it, but don't drink
Broken miner, farmer, waitress, butcher
Greek, Puerto Rican, Croat, Serb, neighborhood
everynight clarinetist same riff
I mean same same samsara same
brick wall for a view
wooden fire escape
across the alley mother screams
at her young ones
"Shaddup you sound like a bunch
of hippies at the park."

Chicago, 1968

LARIMER STREET 1968

7 AM Monday driving to work
out the side window I see
bandaged nicotine damaged
tooth gone hungover haggard
mateless cadaver eyes crawled
out orange crates & freights
plaster falling catacombs
of bottom dollar ruins mustering
on that metal butt prop guard rail
The discards & exiles
The prodigals & residue
of the wild west looking
to jump in the bed of some old
pickup & bend back 10 dollar day

And I'm thinking where
will I be in 88 or 98?
Where are the women?
Where are the sisters of true mercy?
Where have their loves gone?
Why do some prosper and these not?
I know it has little to do with work
Did these guys vote for
the war in Viet Nam?
Did any of these guys vote?
What ambitions remain for them?

What crimes are they ready for?
Why do I feel this bizarre
kinship to these motley ones?

Larimer street where I looked
for somebody else's father
Where I bellowed hobo folk songs
stumbling loaded unrobbed
Where the mythes died like legends
Where as a wet behind the ears
I saw the last gasps of a way
of life, Larimer Street Denver
Collar Ray Dough summer after
the Summer of Love

1968

MOON BURNT STUMBLERS

Black Betty cracking the dawn
the sky strange like dark wine
an entire battalion of moon burnt stumblers
singing don't start jacking off boys
just don't start jacking off
In total fear I ran like Buster Keaton
running from the Keystone Kops
I make Ben Blue eyes and skeedaddle
This is the craziest conglomeration
Their advice is too bizarre for a young
        man or woman for that matter
Their collective breath is making
        flowers wilt, goldfish jump
        out of bowls, cats jump in the lake
        the insect world committing mass
        sepa ku against greasy spoon glass
Their voices full of jagged rocks & broken
        bottles, their wisdom chilling

Sacramento, 1968

The Ballad of Paddy Billikin

Paddy Billikin stepped off the bus
and was greeted by the smell of stale beer
across the street was the pawn shop
the ring in his pocket the cause of his tears
Mary Joe had got knocked up
by a boy from another school
Paddy he was self conscious
all he felt like was a fool
Oceanside had a USO
showers, free pool & TV
John Wayne defeating the "Japs"
almost single handedly
Aldo Ray losing a leg
and still getting the girl
Pinballs skinbooks & gogos
with tassels that twirl

God how it hurt his pride
crankin his guts inside
now she'd never be his bride
1452 miles from Oceanside

It had thousands with clothes hair eyes
just like his & busses that ran too slow

but saddest of all it didn't
have anyone to replace Mary Joe
He read the words of her letter
twisting cold through his cut mind
Deciding that no one loved him
and this life was a waste of time
Now Paddy get hol' of yourself
be a man stand tall
cause after all that training
you're over-sexed under loved
young & mean
you stand tall
you a United States Marine

God how it hurt his pride
crankin his guts inside
now she'd never be his bride
1452 miles from Oceanside

Oakland, 1968

SOLDIERS OF CHRIST

THE DAYS WHEN MY D.I. TOLD US THERE WAS
NO DEMOCRACY IN THE MARINE CORPS
SO OTHERS COULD BE FREE
SO OTHERS COULD HAVE JUSTICE
SO OTHERS COULD HAVE PEACE
WE'D NEVER GET ANY OF IT

It was Sunday at San Diego's MCRD
we Catholics on command formed a detail
for mass
"Protestants" the DI shouted
and all but three formed new ranks
"Jews" he yelled
now only one remained
he paused "Latter Day Saints" he spoke
a decibel lower
"Bewdist?" his eyebrows bunched up
Still one remained
The first sargeant came down off the platform
and put his face 5 inches from the one remaining
"Just what are you pry-vate?"
"Sir, Atheist, Sir!"
the DI sent a short swift deep shot

to the atheist's breadbasket
devastating not from severity
(though a wind destroyer)
but the horribly sad fact
retaliation was totally futile
whatever the DI did was right
"What did you say, maggot?"
the lone one was given no chance to recover
"Protestant," he gasped.
"Protestant, what?" DI demanded.
"Protestant, sir."

San Jose, 1966

MORE ROAD

The radio reports a 22 year old recent college dropout
       of anglo name dressed in beads & full Native
       American headdress stood arms folded in front
       of a speeding locomotive
He made his statement but 22 years from now
       no one will recall in fact not 22
       minutes from now
I'm drinking wine from the 40th century
       a man out of his time!
       shouting more road! more road!
I'm going to try to leave thousands of pages
       as my statement
I'm 22 years old and don't want to die
I wasn't sent here from the 40th century
       to stand in front of a speeding locomotive
       nor to jump from a bridge or skyscraper
I really feel these markings on paper
       justify my going on
       my shouts of more road!

San Jose, 1966

NOTES

40TH CENTURY MAN

1. "The Lost Highway ": song by Leon Payne, bass player in the Drifting Cowboys, Hank Williams' group. Sung by Hank.

2. "Rambling Man": Name of songs by Hank Williams, Allman Brothers, Waylon Jennings.

3. "Roms": what gypsies call themselves

MORE SAME OLD

4. "Christian Identity": militant racist pseudo christian group powerful in Idaho, preach Jews are the spawn of Satan.

ENKIDU RETURNS...

5. "Vacana": form of Bhakti Virasaiva devotional verse (900–1300 AD). Noted Adepts: Basavanna, Devara, Mahadeviyakka, and Allama Prabhu.

6. "Enkidu": The "wild" Other, seduced from the forest by one of Gilgamesh's courtesans. When Enkidu tried to return to the wilds, the other animals and birds no longer understood him, nor he they. Friend, mentor, student of Gilgamesh killed by Bull of Heaven due to a trick of Ishtar. Gilgamesh so loves Enkidu he goes into the Land of Death or Underworld to search for & redeem him, but alas, it is impossible. Gilgamesh is one of our earliest texts.

I SHOULD JOIN UP

7. "Kropotkin": Peter, Anarchist writer, theorist, geographer, publisher, revolutionist.

8. "Emma Goldman": Russian American Socialist Feminist Anarchist who wrote about Kropotkin's de facto imprisonment in the hands of the Bolsheviks after the Revolution.

9. "Tom Paine": imprisoned for being a God-freak in post-revolutionary France & condemned after release for same *Age of Reason* (no second hand revelation) in U.S., for Atheism. *Citizen Tom Paine* by Howard Fast has death scene.

10. "Trumbo, Farmer, Fast, Lowenfels": victims of red scare witch hunt in 40's & early 50's.

11. "AMWAY": quasi-religious, quasi-philosophic, quasi-american, distribution pyramid, teaching materialism as the barometer of worth. Tried to finance 1996 Republican National Convention.

BIG APPLE JUICE

12. "Mojo": Magic fetish, usually in a bag "mojo bag". Gives user sexual power.

13. "John the Conqueror": also John D' Conqueroo. Conquering fetish also an actual spiritual being embodied by the fetish. From New Orleans, and probably West Africa.

14. "Collette": French writer, a "woman's woman's writer"

BEAST

15. "Killer of 12 year old girl": Richard Davis, killer of Polly Klaas. Drawing by Jeanne Boylan preceded identity.

16. "thirst for sand": "A thirst for power is drinking sand" from "Power" by Gregory Corso (*Happy Birthday of Death*).

WAY OUT IN YOU

17. "dakini": In Mahayana Buddhism a consort of the enlightened and those working on it. Spiritual & physical. May take form of bird.
18. "Maitreya": the next buddha (with eschatological overtones)

ACCESS US!

19. "ZAUM": Russian Futurian style language & method. Transrationalism, Beyonsense, The Kitchen Sink, Folk Verse, Pre-Adamic-Evonic enavantic tongue, Jazz, Neologistic, High Energy Manumissing Transmission Concept & Movement. ZA = through, via, transcending, UM = intellect, rationality, convention, perhaps Blake's Urizen.

THIS NOTION

20. Notion for title from Huddie Ledbetter (Leadbelly) song "Goodnight Irene." "Sometimes I get a great notion to take morphine and die" or " jump in the river and drown".
21. "no rifle in mouth": demise of Hemingway.

    "hanging after writing in slit wrist blood": demise of Sergei Essenin, (also spelled Yessenin) immensely popular bad boy imaginist & ruralist Russian poet (Isadora Duncan his 7th wife) who hanged himself in the Hotel Angleterre, Leningrad 1925.

    "losing at russian roulette in Moscow": said to be Mayakovsky's end, 1930. Only one bullet in the chamber, a compulsive gambler, but the suicide note was already written.

    "jumping off bridge in Minneapolis": John Berryman's way out.

22. "It's not over till it's over.": Though oft expressed in ancient & modern poesy, this statement usually attributed to Yogi Berra, baseball player, manager, comedic philosopher.

SEND YOU BACK

23. "Petain": World War I French hero turned Vichy in World War II. Sounds very much like word for slut.

24. "Old Crow": Frank Clausen Jr. brand of blended whiskey from end of World War II till death in early 90's. Sometimes my mother in rage would pour out an entire case. He'd just say "Why you horse's ass you" and go buy another.

AHOJ! MR. PRESIDENT, AHOJ!

25. "Ahoj!": j = y, hence ahoy! Hip ironical greeting in landlocked Czech land.
26. "Mr. President": V. Havel.

27. "Allen": Poet Allen Ginsberg. "Anne": Poet Anne Waldman.

28. "Myshkin": Prince Myshkin, hero?! of Dostoyevsky's *The Idiot.*

29. "pivo": Slav for beer. "pozor": Danger! Beware! Extreme Caution! even Shame!

IMPRESSIONS OF TITOGRAD

30. "Titograd": industrial city (maybe 60,000?) in Montenegro.

31. "family untouched by death in a place like Benares": Buddha told the woman who wanted him to bring her dead child back to life, "Find a family in Benares untouched by death in the last 5 years." She couldn't do it, so Buddha said "bury your child."

UFFIZI LIBATIONS

32. In the Uffizi Spring & Venus are on adjoining walls.

WHAT IMPRESSED ME MOST

33. "As The World Turns": America's longest running TV soap

opera (over 40 years). My mother learned to speak English through this vehicle.

THE BEAR FOR REAL

34. A poem entitled "The Bear" appears in my book *Without Doubt* (Zeitgeist Press). Check A. Ginsberg, "The Lion for Real"

THE STREETS OF KASHI
35. Varanasi, Benares, Kashi, has worn many names.

36. "kirkidum": Indian candy.

37. "Wombi Baba ": Nickname coined by travelling companion. Said I reminded her of a wombat. Affectionately. I think.

38. "bhang": Cannabis prepared for eating or drinking.

   "lassi ": Kefir like yogurt drink.

   "wallah": Working fellow (Dhobi wallah = laundry man).

   "lathi stick": Indian police version of night stick.

   "puja": prayer or offering, also pooja, with many foreign words transliteration is variable, according to individual ear & nationality as even the Western Countries can't agree on phonetics, especially unmetric, AM-PM, harsh a, silent e, weird i, USA.

   "scheduled": post Independence bureaucratic p.c. word for untouchables. The programs inspired by Ghandi Ji were named "scheduled," aiming at democratizing education & end of caste system designation. An affirmative action program.

39. "Ed Sullivan": early television variety show host. Known for distinctive introductions.

GOKYO LAKE

40. "Cho-Oyu": 8,153 meter Majestic Himalayan Mountain overseeing Ngojumba glacier.

41. "shimi-shimi": Tibetan, Sherpa, words for kitty-kitty.

ON THE STREETS OF ELECTRIC NAMCHE

42. "Electric Namche": One of few Nepali mountain towns with electricity (Night time only). A Party & Market town. Home of Tenzing Norgay. (He was there with Hillary, the first time Sagarmatha was ascended.) I motion we call the highest solid substance attached to earth Sagarmatha "Mother or perhaps Goddess of the Universe", not the name of a British surveyor, put *it* in the parentheses. We stayed in rough hewn room where Jimmy Carter had slept. A picture of Jimmy's trek group above the bed.

43. "Tashi Delek" pronounced tashidelay means good fortune. I read this a recent development, because Tibetan has no equivalent of hello. They just get on with it.

44. "zopkyos ": half yak— half buff

LUBLICKLA

45. "Lublickla ": For me to know and you to find out.

46. "Elana Guro": Russian Futurian. Quiet. Similar in "feel" to E. Dickinson. Awesome.

OUR CONCEPTIONS, OUR CHILDREN

47. "Asokan": (often Ashokan) Asoka = B.C. Buddhist king or emperor of part of India who inaugurated a time of hospital, road, sewer, old folk's homes, building. Was careful to make distinction between his personal belief in Buddhism and his job as unbiased emperor. Yet he is often associated with the Third Council of Buddhism, where Theravadas decided to exclude dissidents & innovators which later caused the schism into Little & Greater Vehicles. Asoka's writings never mention the Pataliputra 250 B.C. council and exclusion would seem out of character. The empire lasted close to 500 years. Asoka propagated Dhamma or Dharma. These unifying principles were acceptable to people of any sect. The fundamentals were: Toleration, non-violence, and welfare of all the people.

LEGS OF WINE

48. "Blue Angel": Movie starring Marlene Dietrich. Later version starring May Britt. Young woman drives older professor nuts.

THE DECONSTRUCTION OF AN ERECTION

49. Anecdote about Blok from Mayakovsky's autobiography, *Me, Myself.*

50. "Tsvetayeva": Marina, Russian Poet, (1892–1941) returned to Russia in 1938 before the war; husband Sergei Efron shot for "political unreliability," her son killed in first weeks of war, her daughter sent to a concentration camp, on August 31, 1941 in Elabuga, Marina hung herself.

51. Cost of Nancy Reagan's new china reported at 220 thousand dollars (1984).

JESUS ON HORSEBACK 4 JULY

52. "Stray Dog Cafe": Russian poets' hangout in the 19teens. Petersburg.

WATCHING MY BREATH IN CV

53. "Cassidy": First born son. Tried to name him after Neal and spelled it incorrectly. Anthropologist. Great Friend.

54. "Reich": Wilhelm, revolutionary sexual political psychologist.

GUTENBERG'S BIBLE

55. "Peter Doyle": Livery Driver, companion & love of Walt Whitman. Known as no. 131 in Whitman's notes scolding himself on his "adhesiveness."

56. "Anne Gilchrist": English poet & scholar, who developed crush on Walt Whitman. Told him she was the woman in "A Woman Waits for Me". Came all the way from England.

BIG TIME BEAUCOUP TOKE

57. "Beaucoup": All purpose positive adjective picked up by Nam vets during War.

58. "Alchuringa": Australoid-Aboriginal spirits waiting in holy spots like watering holes to be freed or born into life by the proper actions of people.

59. "Tovarisch": brotherly, on the road together.

FAILURE

60. "Kronstadt": city where aprox. 10,000 sailors, dock workers & sympathizers, history has named anarchists, were massacred after an uprising strike that came about because as they exported the grain families back home farmed, letters from home came describing famine. Trotsky was the general over-seer of the putdown & suppression.

TESTICLES

61. "ambitious genius buddy" became TV writer of renown, intro-duced sweat to bedroom scenes among other things. Proof a good guy can make a good living writing in America.

62. "The Corps": U.S. Marine Corps.

DOGSHIT

63. "muff diving": cunnilingus & if you needed to know this, I probably should explain Forbidden Fruit and what Eve & Adam's Apple symbolizes?

THEY ARE COMING

64. "Bergmann movies": Ingmar Bergmann great Swedish Filmmaker. Movie I allude to starred Liv Ullman. Two college girls sitting in the seat in back of us were unabashedly digi-tizing themselves.

ALL THIS PAINTING

65. "Pachuco": Post-WW II Mexican-American rebel & outlaw movement & style.

66. "Red Irish Oakland Bar" Actually just inside Berkeley, "The Starry Plough".

START THE SUN

67. "Al ": dear friend Al Vla.

DIABLO

68. "Joaquin Murrieta": Californian Robin Hood.

LENNY

69. "crank": also crink as in chicken crink, outlaw kitchen sink methedrine, sometimes used to cover the USP kind. "Meth" was a favorite of Hitler, Peggy the Pistol, some outlaw bikers, Larry Clark's Tulsa, my late brother Phillip.

SONG OF THE SISKIYOU

70. "hand muzzled first cry": such a scene described in Mari Sandoz' *Cheyenne Autumn*.

71. "jalopy" yesteryear slang for hooptie.

LITTLE WALTER IN EUGENE

72. Little Walter was a blues singer & giant of the harmonica famous for chromatic harp (having a valve for sharps & flats). Made it sound like a saxophone.

THE NIGHT I HEARD KEROUAC DIED

73. "Green Chain": chain-operated delivery system of just-cut wood, either sheets of veneer to make plywood or as on this

one big pieces of lumber, some foot high-- foot wide 24 footers (hemlock & spruce). The green-chain hands pull the wood off into carts or skids (palettes) according to size and grade as it comes by on the chain. Here my job was to pull off the unfit wood to go in the chipper (instead of to Japan) to make chip-board. In a veneer plant the lead man calls out the grade "heart!" or "sap!" or "white speck!" which is that dark, semi-eaten wood, the inside plies of your everyday plywood. It can be a very athletic job; if you stay long enough bursitis & carpal & all those are certain.

74. Many references to works by Kerouac & Ginsberg. Desolation Angels refers to Kerouac's name for his buddies in book of same title.

GANDY DANCING MONTANA

75. "gandy dancing": Railroad pick & shovel hand. The gandy dance is a way with the short shovel to get gravel under the new or replaced tie to "tamp it up" (make it level). It looks funny, one leg does it. I can still do it.

76. "Pat Brady ": young friend student of Neal Cassady.

LARIMER STREET 68

77. "mythes": I used the obsolete spelling of myth because in my tenderfoot age I thought this was a superb reference to the deemed obsolete hobo.

MOON BURNT STUMBLERS

78. "Black Betty ": slave nickname for whip.

THE BALLAD OF PADDY BILLIKIN

79. "Paddy Billikin": both names for hick white guys. "Paddy-dude" used by SF Bay Area Chicanos & Originals, probably from the old moniker for immigrant Irish.

LOOKING BACK ON THE END OF THE WORLD   Kamper & Wulf, eds.
THE LOST DIMENSION   Paul Virilio
LUSITANIA   JOURNAL OF REFLECTION & OCEANOGRAPHY   Martim Avillez, ed.
THE MADAME REALISM COMPLEX   Lynne Tillman
MAGPIE REVERIES   THE ICONOGRAPHIC MANDALAS OF James Koehnline
MARX BEYOND MARX   LESSONS ON THE GRUNDRISSE   Antonio Negri
THE MEDIA ARCHIVE   Foundation for the Advancement of Illegal Knowledge
METATRON   THE RECORDING ANGEL   Sol Yurick
MIDNIGHT OIL   WORK, ENERGY, WAR, 1973–1992   Midnight Notes Collective
MILLENNIUM   Hakim Bey
MODEL CHILDREN   INSIDE THE REPUBLIC OF RED SCARVES   Paul Thorez
THE MOTHER OF GOD   Luna Tarlo
THE NARRATIVE BODY   Eldon Garnet
NEW ENCLOSURES   Midnight Notes Collective
THE NEW FUCK YOU   ADVENTURES IN LESBIAN READING   Eileen Myles & Liz Kotz, eds.
NOMADOLOGY: THE WAR MACHINE   Gilles Deleuze & Félix Guattari
NOT ME   Eileen Myles
OASIS   Maliqalim Simone, et al., eds.
ON THE LINE   Gilles Deleuze & Félix Guattari
THE ORIGIN OF *THE* SPECIES   Barbara BArg
PIONEER OF INNER SPACE   THE LIFE OF FITZ HUGH LUDLOW   Donald P. Dulchinos
PIRATE UTOPIAS   MOORISH CORSAIRS & CHRISTIAN RENEGADOES   Peter Lamborn Wilson
THE POLITICS OF TRUTH   Michel Foucault
POLYSEXUALITY   François Peraldi, ed.
POPULAR DEFENSE & ECOLOGICAL STRUGGLES   Paul Virilio
PURE WAR   Paul Virilio & Sylvère Lotringer
PSYCHEDELICS REIMAGINED   Thomas Lyttle, ed.
RACE TRAITOR   TREASON TO WHITENESS IS LOYALTY TO HUMANITY   Noel Ignatiev & John Garvey, eds.
RADIOTEXT(E)   Neil Strauss, Dave Mandl, et al.
READING BROOKE SHIELDS   THE GARDEN OF FAILURE   Elden Garnet
RED TAPE   TRAGICOMICS   Michael Carter, ed.
REMARKS ON MARX   CONVERSATIONS WITH DUCCIO TROMBADORI   Michel Foucault
RETHINKING MARXISM   ESSAYS FOR HARRY MAGDOFF & PAUL SWEEZY   S. Resnick & R. Wolff, eds.
THE ROOT IS MAN   Dwight Macdonald
THE ROTTING GODDESS   CLASSICAL ORIGINS OF THE WITCH   Jacob Rabinowitz
SADNESS AT LEAVING   Erje Ayden
SCANDAL   ESSAYS IN ISLAMIC HERESY   Peter Lamborn Wilson
SEMIOTEXT(E) ARCHITECTURE   Hraztan Zeitlian, ed.
SEMIOTEXT(E) SF   Rudy Rucker, Robert Anton Wilson & Peter Lamborn Wilson, eds.
SEMIOTEXT(E) USA   Jim Fleming & Peter Lamborn Wilson, eds.
SHEROES & WOMYN WARRIORS CALENDAR   O.R.S.S.A.S.M.
SHOWER OF STARS   THE INITIATIC DREAM IN SUFISM & TAOISM   Peter Lamborn Wilson
SICK BURN CUT   Deran Ludd
SIMULATIONS   Jean Baudrillard
69 WAYS TO PLAY THE BLUES   Jürg Laederach
SOCIAL OVERLOAD   Henri-Pierre Jeudy
SOCIETY OF THE SPECTACLE & OTHER FILM SCRIPTS   Guy Debord
SOFT SUBVERSIONS   Félix Guattari
SOUNDING OFF   MUSIC AS RESISTANCE / SUBVERSION / REVOLUTION   Sakolsky & Ho, eds.
SPEED AND POLITICS   AN ESSAY ON DROMOLOGY   Paul Virilio
STILL BLACK, STILL STRONG   Dhoruba bin Wahad, Mumia Abu-Jamal, Assata Shakur
STREET POSTERS & BALLADS OF THE LOWER EAST SIDE   Eric Drooker
T.A.Z.   THE TEMPORARY AUTONOMOUS ZONE, ONTOLOGICAL ANARCHY, POETIC TERRORISM   Hakim Bey
THIS IS YOUR FINAL WARNING!   Thom Metzger
THIS WORLD WE MUST LEAVE   Jacques Camatte
THE TOUCH   Michael Brownstein
TROTSKYISM & MAOISM   A. Belden Fields
THE UNBEARABLES   The Unbearables
THE UNHOLY BIBLE   HEBREW LITERATURE OF THE KINGDOM PERIOD   Jacob Rabinowitz
WALKING THROUGH CLEAR WATER IN A POOL PAINTED BLACK   Cookie Mueller
WHORE CARNIVAL   Shannon Bell, ed.
WIGGLING WISHBONE   PATASEXUAL SPECULATIONS   Bart Plantenga
WILD CHILDREN   Dave Mandl & Peter Lamborn Wilson, eds.
X-TEXTS   Derek Pell
XXX FRUIT   XXX Fruit Collective
¡ZAPATISTAS!   Subcommandante Marcos & Members of the Emiliano Zapata Liberation Movement